MOTHERS

AN ENDANGERED SPECIES

SUSAN CHIOFALO

VAC PUBLISHING

Dedicated to my four children who gave me all the material for this book and much, much more.

CONTENTS

CHAPTER 1

THE POWER BEHIND THE THRONE

My mother, the Queen of Detergent, married a commoner with a congenital deficiency towards disinfectant. Together, they sired me, the Pig Princess, and my two younger brothers, the Duke of Dirt and the Squire of Slovene. In our castle, which graced the Hamlet known as Astoria in the Township of Queens, New York, mother reigned supreme over cleanliness and godliness. She waged daily battle with her arch enemies, Filth and Grime, who were no match for her arsenal of cleansing weapons.

The royal lineage however, proved a bit disappointing to Her Majesty, who tried desperately to convince them that the only way to maintain both royalty and sanity was through sanitation. "Clean of body, clean of mind!", she would pontificate repeatedly. To us, this meant that she was about to scrub our brains out. We made hasty retreat.

Early on, my mother discovered the formula for elbow grease and dispensed it liberally. Elbow grease, we quickly learned, is the only compound that will "get the job done". It is all the more valuable because it is completely invisible, and leaves no residue. As soon as she noticed us slowing down in our appointed chores, mom would come after us and bellow, "rub on some more elbow grease!". Another thing that we noticed about this magical compound is that it is free. Mom was never one to waste a penny either.

Mom put the laundry on a steady diet of spray starch, and took pride in ironing our socks. She fluffed all our cloth diapers, and continued to do so even after they were recycled into dust rags. She viewed permanent press as a personal affront, as it usurped some of her power. Who were garment manufacturers to compete with her iron? How would they like her to straighten out a few wrinkles in their thinking?

It was my brother who started the rumor that the iron had nested in one of our suitcases and had a baby in there. Sure enough, while on our next vacation, mom reached into her valise and triumphantly pulled out a miniature of the one that stood as a fixture on the ironing board in our kitchen. Like all infants, it required a lot of attention. And from that time on, mom spent part of each vacation day "bumping down" articles of our clothing along with those hotel sheets and towels that did not live up to her standards.

Dishes gave birth overnight in the sink, and the new offspring always had to be washed and wiped. Mother's dishes were so clean that you could see your face in her Mel Mac. Our bathroom was as picture perfect as a suite in a hotel brochure. The toilet received the royal attention due The Throne. It was a well-known fact that mom kept a big bald man in a bottle right behind that throne. This man possessed cleansing powers beyond our comprehension. Believe me, whenever any of us used the bathroom, we kept a very careful eye on that bottle, just in case that bald man should take offense to our business in there and suddenly appear before we were finished using the toilet. From Monday through Thursday mom dusted and scrubbed. By Friday everything had to be in order for our cleaning lady.

Alas, her endeavors on our behalves were in vain. Mother could not get us, me, in particular, to clean up my act. One day in exasperation, the Queen of Detergent summoned Marvin her Magician, and ordered him to cast a spell upon me. It was divined that I should one day marry, and sire a pig such as myself. As it turns out, Marvin was not your ordinary genie in a bottle. He was the industrial strength one that lived in a drum. He was also an overachiever at sorcery. And so it came to pass that in due time I married and had not one, but four piglets. In order to even up the score however, I sent my brood over to visit with mom and dad regularly, thus restoring filth and squalor to their castle.

The moral of the story is this. Given the ability to set the curse of the ages upon your children, just remember how that can backfire. You really want to be careful how you wield that sort of power.

CHAPTER 2

THE MATERNAL OLYMPICS

I was brought up in the same farmhouse that both my mother and my grandmother before her were born in. Apparently, poverty forced that side of the family to continually recycle names. Everyone shared names such as August (or Augusta), William (or Wilhelmina), Erich (Erika), and Alma. This must have been very difficult for poor old great-aunt Augusta who had eight kids.

The fact that my grandma had married an extremely wealthy man never interfered with her penchant for frugality. On the kitchen window sill sat a hand carved imported flower vase that contained a mixture of water and all the old slivers of soap bars that the family had used. Nobody ever knew what she actually did with that gooey mess, but it was as sacred to the family as a burial urn as it sat glistening in the sunshine in the priceless container.

Grandma turned her gift for recycling into a thriving enterprise, and thus initiating me into the world of big business. She squirreled away all of our old newspapers under the front porch in what was formerly the coal bin. She saved the used strings from the butcher and bakery wrap to bundle up these papers periodically and we would pull it on my red wagon to a recycling center where she got 2 cents a bundle. With this money we shared a Charlotte Ruse, purchased in our local shopping district. Never would it have dawned on me to ask for my own treat, and risk being admonished as a "spendthrift". Never mind the fact that the shopping district was built on property that my grandfather had once owned and sold before he died, thereby increasing grandma's fortune.

Grandma, never heard of electrons, was suspicious of electricity, and never installed a telephone in the house. Instead, she would walk down to the corner bar going through the "ladies entrance" to make a phone call. She always took a small glass container with her and would pay the bartender a "couple cents" to fill it with beer. Buying a bottle of beer would have cost extra for the bottle. And one had to find the means to put "food and drink" on the table.

Aside from our weekly visits to the cemetery to clean up and decorate the grave sites, house cleaning was grandma's interest, her hobby and her raison d'être. Her stove was without a smudge, without a footprint from the army of cockroaches that marched across it daily. Grandma refused to even acknowledge their existence. "Bugs come from old newspapers" she would insist (big business carries its liabilities). Her bedpan could double as a mirror during the day. Her hand starched lace curtains stood up by themselves and saluted as you passed by our windows. She tied towels to my mother's knees as a baby, so that as she crawled, she would simultaneously clean the floors.

This was too good a challenge for my mother, as an adult to ignore. If grandma could wash a wall, mom could scrub the paint off of it. If grandma could polish the silver, mom could render it in need of re-plating. If grandma could clean a floor, mom could resurface it. The Maternal Olympics was on! Then, in the last quarter of the Dust bowl, mom hit a touch-down. While grandma had one child, mom had three. While grandma birthed hers at home, mom had hers in the maternity ward at the local hospital thus maintaining spotless sheets at home during delivery. And so the dust cap had been handed down.

It was in this house that I was raised, believing that the planets circled the sun secondarily, and that I was the true center of the universe. Everything in my little world had to be perfect. My clothes were hand stitched. My sheets and pillowcases had to have hand crocheted borders. Cinderella would have drooled over my carriage. Visitors were screened at the door for germs. I was formula fed because mom could put *those* nipples in the sterilizer.

From PIT (Princess in Training) I graduated to full JAP (Jewish American Princess) with storybook ease and grace. To spare me from acne, my mother hired people to go through puberty for me. I accepted this adoration with aplomb. As a full princess, I ruled our household firmly, yet benevolently. I allowed oxygen, if not space, for my two brothers who came after me.

Despite quite high SAT scores, it was rumored in fifth grade that I was retarded because I still did not dress myself. A disability I might add, which my own children point out persists to this very day. As I entered young adulthood, I was "totally independent", although I lived at home on my parent's income. I was "cool" because I was "different", although I dressed like all my friends, listened to the same music and spoke the same "lingo". I was the "Everyone Else" who made other parent's life miserable. In order to secure my financial future, I was enrolled in a private college in Brooklyn to study medical students whose fathers might leave them a thriving medical practice. While others of my generation smoked pot and demonstrated against the government, I caused my mother a terrifying brush with failure when I announced my decision to abandon the brilliant career in scientific research that she had chosen for me, and marry my childhood sweetheart.

Mother's feudal commitment to me did not end there. As my husband and I moved clear across the country, this loyal subject dragged my father along with her determined to fulfill her parental obligation to me and help develop independent grandchildren. When I had my first child, she convinced me that I had invented labor pains.

CHAPTER 3

THE TORCH IS PASSED-AGAIN

In the Maternal Olympics, mom finished as easy first. Here was a woman who could spend the first half of New Year's Eve in the emergency room having a rubber mouse's tail removed from her son's ear, and the other half dancing like Cinderella at the ball. Mom was Snow White tidying up the cottage of her adorable but messy little dwarfs. She won the gold and passed the torch down to me. It was clear to me that my job was to prime a few hopefuls of my own.

I raised all four of our children as "firsts". I carried each of them an extra month just to be sure that they were completely ready for this world. To bring order to their home life, we named them in alphabetical order and posted A,B,C, and D on their bedroom doors. Or maybe that was for me. As babies, we reveled in the fact that they could eliminate on their own. We basked in the glow of their achievements. We studied every distinct sound that our babies uttered, so that we could reproduce them in telephone calls to our relatives and friends. On the other hand (and you can trust me on this) when one of baby's first words is "dammit", this is not cause to run to the tape recorder.

Because I quickly fulfilled my children's every wish, need and desire, before they even had one, none of them spoke full sentences before entering kindergarten. I served them breakfast in bed on trays every morning, after opening the blinds only slightly so as not to shock them from their angelic slumber into reality too suddenly. While the children enjoyed their morning programs on television propped up on their newly fluffed pillows, I packed four different lunches in order to fortify them enough to survive their arduous day sitting at their desks and snacking in the playground.

I raised our children to believe that there was a dust fairy that kept their rooms clean and tidy. Where their garments were stored was a well guarded secret since I laid out all their outfits for them. I spent the first weekend of every month weeding out their toy boxes. We hired a nanny for them, and I competed with her in marathon song and story telling sessions. We encouraged our children to be artistic and creative. They took music lessons, art lessons, and dancing lessons. On Sunday evenings we had them entertain our dinner guests. It never dawned upon us that only parents and grandparents consider "Piano Exercises for Young Fingers" after dinner entertainment. Everyone else considers it payment in full for the meal.

My husband and I took turns at being the Easter Bunny, Santa Claus, the Tooth Fairy, and the children's activity director on vacations. In order to ensure our children's popularity, I became the neighborhood Pied Piper and ran a soup kitchen as well. It was routine to have ten or so children at our table for home made "garbage soup" for lunch on a cold winter day. For some moms this was a difficult thing to swallow, until I reluctantly shared my recipe for leftover vegetables. When I was hungry I fed my kids. When I was cold I put extra clothes on them. Of course, as I piled clothing on the kids, my husband, whose thermostat has been broken ever since he fell off his rocker, began to methodically remove them. Is it any wonder that to this day they never know whether they should be hot or cold, and that they change outfits ten times a day?

On Wednesdays I played Uber driver. I would pick the kids up at school at 3 PM, drop C & D at religious instruction, A to baseball practice, and B to dance, clear across to the other side of town. I would arrive back in time to pick up C&D from religion, drop C at soccer practice, and D at home to start her homework. I would drop in at a friend's house before picking up A, B & C, and rushing home to start supper. Zoe was usually flopped out by her pool with her head behind a woman's magazine.

"I still don't understand how some women can hold a full time job, have children who wear matching socks to school, live in homes that don't appear as though the big one has already hit, and still have enough reason to put on perfume at night," she would lament. "Either they have found a time warp somewhere, or they are androids and don't require sleep."
"Maybe they exercise. I hear it's good for energy" I replied.
"Exercise! As if housework wasn't painful enough! Oh yea, I read about that all the time. Organize, prioritize, and exercise! It's a load of verbal excrement."

"It sells magazines," I answered, flipping through hers to see if I could pick up any quick pointers.

Years ago Zoe implemented several "time saving measures" around her household. She stopped dusting, insisting that dusting was merely a relocation of dust particles from one place to another. She stopped making beds when she heard a woman at the supermarket remark that if she didn't make hers in the morning, she couldn't think straight all day.
"Imagine what happens to this poor woman's mind on moving day", she whispered to me.
"It's too horrible to dwell upon," I reassured her.
Fingers replaced utensils in her house. "Children naturally do better with their fingers anyway", she pointed out to me. "And it's

more like eating out to them."

Paper plates soon replaced the standard ironstone. The thought that these plates might just be worth more than what she was serving on them made me a little uneasy. Growing in Zoe's refrigerator are new life forms just waiting to be discovered. Way in the back of her vegetable drawer is a piece of limp vegetation with so much hair on it that it resembles a tiny mammal. I didn't have the heart to disturb it. In case it might be molting. One day while I was there, her son wandered into the room to rummage through for a snack.

"Hey mom! How old is this salsa?" he inquired about a pulpy red substance with brown spots floating on the top.

"How should I know?" she answered. "How long have we lived here?"

"Can I have this kiwi?" he asked, holding up a fuzzy greenish spherical object.

"I think that was a lime at one time". I said. I grabbed it from him, just before he sliced into it.

Zoe's medicine cabinets boast an assortment of leftover prescription pills, dried up under-arm deodorants, and leaky tubes of hemorrhoid preparations. A herd of wooly balls roam across the prairie of her kitchen floor daily to their corral under the dishwasher. There is a note on her refrigerator to remind her take her pre-natal vitamins, although her youngest is seven. On weekends at Zoe's house, one glass of wine could sometimes lead directly to another, which would lead us to the inevitable game of "Confidential". In this game, Zoe would usually open with some startling confession that I had to try to top, or at least keep a secret from the rest of our little world.

"I had breast implants five years ago", she would boast.

"I ran out of WD-40 again and had to use vegetable oil on our front door handle", I countered, knowing that I was losing miserably right out the gate.

"I had an affair with the small appliance salesman in Smart-Mart that lasted one whole month"! She was really getting good at this game.

"No way! The tall dark one with the green eyes? I bought an electric can opener from him!"

In Zoe's bedroom there is a drawer marked "Adults Only" in which she and her husband keep all their "off limits stuff". She showed it to me once during a game of "Confidential". It is a truly remarkable collection of battery operated and exotic gizmos that keep their sex life pumping right along.

I have an "Adult Only" drawer too. It's in the kitchen and contains my collection of bread twists, razor blades, a rubber band ball, my restaurant matchbook collection, a metal shoe horn, two firecrackers that I wrangled from our son's hand on July 4th 1990, a package of three metal coat and hat hooks and a sliding door pin that we never installed when we bought the house 9 years ago. Under that, a plate hanger for a 7"-10" decorative plate, sticks of plant food, a valence rod extension, a piece of wood that broke off my desk fifteen years ago, three plug-in air fresheners, assorted screws nuts and bolts that bolted out of some appliance or piece of furniture, the cat's hair ball malt (which I doubt she will need in heaven), a rusty lock and key set which belongs on the back gate, the lid from the butter compartment from some past refrigerator, a box of Christmas tree ornament hangers, tiny vials of assorted colors of glitter, several sizes of felt pads for chair legs, and a few electrical plates from wall outlets covered with various wallpaper patterns. My mother once tried to dispose of the entire contents of this drawer when she went in there to find a flashlight battery, and stumbled upon my stash of our four children's baby teeth and someone's dried up umbilical cord. But I know that the minute I throw anything out, I will need it.

In a way, Zoe is my hero. She gave birth to both of her children at home, in her own bathtub. Mom says that Zoe is my alter-ego. Maybe, but my dominant personality is definitely Martha Stewart.

CHAPTER 4

AMAZING GRACE

On the other side of town from our house, my husband's Italian Catholic family lived on the same block as their church. His mother attended mass there every Sunday without fail. Vince, my future husband, played stickball with the same priest who baptized him, and gave him first Holy Communion and Confirmation. It was his mother's dearest wish that this same priest would someday marry Vince to some nice Italian girl who could give him good Marinara sauce and give her lots of Catholic grandchildren. And so, she prayed.

His mother worried about her three boys. She worried about them not being accepted here in America. She wouldn't allow Italian to be spoken at home. She worried that they were short. She fed them well. She worried that they had too many cavities. She sent them to an expensive dentist. She worried that they got in trouble at school. She spent much time in the principal's office. She worried that they needed more money for the boy's music lessons and a summer home in Atlantic City, NJ. She went out to work. She worried about her son's religious commitments. She put them all in catechism classes after school. And she prayed.

Vince had other worries at this time. He worried that he would get caught playing hooky from his catechism class again. He worried that he would not get to rendezvous with his girlfriend behind the church during that hour of instruction to feel up her breasts. He worried, as a matter of fact, that he would run out of girlfriends in his own neighborhood before he could get his driver's license and start cruising other neighborhoods. The Italian Stallion didn't have to worry for long. When he was twelve years old, he met me.

Time passed. My future mother-in-law went to church and prayed. She prayed for Vince, her youngest son who was interested in a Jewish girl. She prayed for his grades and his musical talents, neither of which he seemed to show any interest in any more. She prayed that he would not stray from what he had learned during the time that she had sent him to catechism class. Her prayers were answered. He hadn't.

Vince had other problems to worry about. He had to worry about getting a job after school to make enough money to take me out. He worried about other boys flirting with me, and about me flirting back. He worried that he couldn't afford to get a car so that we could make out in the drive-in movies. He worried that my parents would find out that we did and would not let me see him again. He need not have worried. They did anyway.

Time passed. On Saturday nights Vince and his brothers shared a whiskey at the corner bar with their priest. My future mother-in law went to church and prayed. She prayed for her two eldest sons who were in the service, and for her youngest son who might get drafted to fight in Vietnam if he didn't stay in college. She prayed that all the boys would get married before their girlfriends got pregnant, and in order of seniority in big church weddings. She prayed that her youngest son would not marry a Jewish girl who would name her grandchildren names such as Gittel, Sol and Yentel. She didn't have a prayer.

Vince worried that he couldn't keep up his grades in college, hold a full-time job, and date me at the same time. He worried that I was dating Jewish boys from my college who were going on to medical school. He worried because my roommate was getting married after graduation in June, and that I might want to do the same. He worried about how to afford a larger diamond engagement ring than she got.

Time passed. My future mother-in-law went to church and prayed that God was not angry with her youngest son for having married a Jewish girl. She prayed that I would settle down, put my career on hold, and start a family. She prayed that her grandsons would outnumber the granddaughters, and that the family name would be carried on. She prayed for her sons, that they could afford to buy their families houses in nice communities on the same block as their churches. She prayed that her grandchildren would come back to the church, and go to Sunday Mass.

Vince had other worries. He worried how we were ever going to finish paying for the wedding album and for the caterers. He worried that he couldn't afford to finish graduate school and pay for my education as well. He worried about furniture payments, car payments and that we were going to have to move in with his parents while we saved for a house. He worried that he was going bald with all this worry. No sense in worrying. He was.

Time passed. While my mother-in-law prayed, miracles began to occur. Her boys came home from the service and got married. Everyone bought their own houses, furniture and cars. Even her youngest son and his Jewish wife had four children. There were grandsons to carry on the family name. There were granddaughters to worry about. They were all short, got cavities and went to school and catechism classes. All three sons and their families began to attend Sunday Mass. Their wives taught Sunday school. I became Catholic and Vince became a Eucharistic Minister. My mother-in-law became a Saint.

CHAPTER 5

TROUBLE ALWAYS COMES IN THREES

The year is 16AD, which stands for 16 years After Donna. In 16 years Maid Miserable had perfected her gift for demanding the impossible. Somehow this child could sense the exact moment that the very last drop of ice cream had been licked out of the bowl. That's when she would develop ice-cream withdrawal symptoms, and ravage the freezer looking for some. She might have been in school all day, but she would know that I had just spent my last dime on paper diapers. As she emerged from the school bus the first thing that she would say is that she lost her gym sneakers and needed a new pair. If I had spent the day in the kitchen cooking a gourmet meal, she would crave pizza. She would get a sudden urge to take her siblings to see a movie on the very day that they were on restriction. When I wanted her to take them, she had a ton of homework to do.

Maid Miserable had developed her psychic abilities to the point where she was in full control of the entire community. She could predict when a store would be out of a particular brand of anything. Even the forces of nature were no match for this prophet. If it rained, she would have set aside that afternoon to get a tan. If it hit 100 degrees in the shade, she would have wanted to work on her track record. I don't know if this sort of talent is inherited, but

God help us all if this sort of clairvoyance can be taught.

After the first day of high school one year, she announced,
"I hate school and I'm never going back!"
"Good for you" I shouted back, "One must always move forward!"
"And to top it off", she added, "I'm the shortest girl in third period class!"
"And who won for tallest?" I inquired, apparently totally engaged.
On the way out of the bathroom, she informed the dog "Damn! I just got another zit!"
"Have you introduced it to the others?" I replied.
"New additions are not always planned, nor are they always pleasant" I sagely advised, hoping that she would catch the double meaning.
"And by the way, one of the greatest lies of all times is that pregnancy cures acne!" I added, hoping that she would catch the only meaning.

Our second teenager arrived gift wrapped as a baby. Hidden behind her cherubic cheeks and her angelic smile was a calculator with a built in camera. By the time she got home from the hospital and got tucked into her basinet, she had photographed our possessions, calculated our approximate financial worth, and decided how much allowance to ask for. At least with the first one, we knew what we had from the time she could speak. This one had us all fooled. She only seemed to float through life like a bubble on a breeze, oblivious to the world. Little did we know that she had put her brain on autopilot in order to attend to more pressing matters. Like what kind of car she should ask for and what her percentage of the inheritance would be worth in seventy years.

Teenager number two could function perfectly well in this world, while we sincerely suspected that a brain monitor would indicate zero activity going on in there. I clearly remember the day, while reading a magazine, she asked me what "post humorously" meant.

"I believe that is posthumously", I replied.

"What is?" she questioned, in a rather vaporized state.

"What you are trying to say" I replied, checking her ability to dilate.

"I don't get it" came the reply.

"What I'm trying to tell you is that you are confusing two different words. Posthumously means after one dies. Humorously means funny".

"That's sad mom", she said snapping back into reality.

"Why so?"

"Because it's rude to make fun of someone who is dead!" she replied indignantly.

We used to call her The Dutchess of Disorder, believing that her bedroom was the mirror of her mind, reflecting her thoughts, which were so cluttered with nonsense that she could not possibly find a thing in there that made any sense whatsoever. How could we know that this child, like her older sister would go on to become a medical professional. If only we had a crystal ball. Or a housekeeper.

We had a short reprieve from girls with our son, and then Lady Sarah Heartburn was born, addicted to Sesame Street and Mr. Roger's Neighborhood. And although there is no truth in the rumor that she was injected with a phonograph needle at birth, she would break into a song at the drop of a note. Furthermore, she believed everything she saw on a 25 inch screen with absolute conviction. One day, on my way through the family room I noticed her sitting mesmerized by the TV set, her little hand held high in the air. "Raise your hand if you're sure!" the deodorant commercial sang. She was sure.

Bonnie entered emotional puberty before kindergarten. It was my fault , of course that she was a born survivor. After four kids in six years, the crib was not the only one on it's last leg. Bonnie practically diapered and nursed herself. At the age of five, she insisted on a pre-training bra. Imprinting on her older sisters, she also started training her hair to develop a chemical dependency to all advertised hair products. I thought that having been trained by the other two girls I might have the advantage over this child.

"Generic Shampoo does not cause head lice!" I repeated over and over. "Mirrors don't need hairspray buildup any more than you do!" I would plead. Too late; She had already been indoctrinated into the First Commandment of Puberty by her sisters. "**Any teenager who doesn't resent parental advice lacks character and is a wimp**".

It was in kindergarten that we noticed that she had stopped wearing clothes, preferring to outfit herself from the costume box in the attic. One day she would be Wonder Woman, the next Star Bright, and the next a ballerina. Here was a child who could make a costume out of a pillowcase, a one inch hunk of left over elastic and a hand-full of sequins. She hoarded paper crowns from fast food restaurants. She glittered and wore any of my high heels that she could get her hands on. I remember approaching her kindergarten teacher on the subject.
"Have you noticed lately that one of your students has been dressing like a wino?" I inquired timidly.
"Well, if you mean Bonnie, she certainly is a fashion statement", came the cautious reply.
"I hope you don't think that I am responsible for this" I tried to appear slightly appalled. "As a matter of fact, we have a British nanny who gets our children ready for school, and I had no idea that this was going on", I half-lied indignantly.
"That explains the Queen of England outfit", she replied.

By the time she was eight and a half, our last baby started locking her bedroom door, and spent hours in there watching old tapes of musical theater productions. She would appear fleetingly at intervals in the kitchen, her head buried in the refrigerator contemplating an attack on the more vulnerable eye-level snacks. Then she would notice her shadow, and quickly retreat to her burrow.

"What are you up to in there? Are you hungry dear"? I would call in sweetly, with little hope for a reply.

"Nothing and no!", she would yell back. It's amazing how much time and energy it takes these kids to do nothing. God created the world and all the creatures in it in less time. Even Rome, which we all know was not built in a day, didn't take a fraction of the time it takes the average teenager to accomplish absolutely zap.

Maybe it's because I spent so much time reading up on progressive parenting that I didn't have much time left to practice on her. But Bonnie grew up as much a product of the movies and the stage performances that she watched, as she was a product of us. At other times I convince myself that she was just naturally born to open presents and get her bikini hairs waxed.

CHAPTER 6

NOT A GHOST OF A CHANCE

Adam should have been born an armadillo. Mere skin was not enough to protect this child from his environment. After a twenty-minute labor, he shot out of me like a football. Our obstetrician caught him in mid-air. His dad was still pulling up his surgical outfit during the episiotomy. At that point I was in no position to understand the full seriousness of the situation.

From eight to eleven years of age, Adam was too busy producing hybrid bicycles; taking apart perfectly good ones to use for parts, to concern himself with anything as mundane as reality. The Prince of Pliers had a collection of cross-matched vehicles that would make Dr. Mendel drool with envy. The American Kennel Association should only be so successful with their crossbreeds. The "Surf and Turf" for instance, was a surfboard mounted on top of roller skates. It was not only road worthy, it became amphibian when necessary. His "Scooter-cycle" could reach supersonic speeds and carried a parachute for deceleration. The main requirement of his rolling museum of wreckage is that they be fast. If the Dept. of Motor Vehicles ever got wind of some of his inventions, they'd require registration and a license.

Like many boys his age, our son kept a ghost in his bedroom closet. This explains why his clothes were never at home there, but were hysterically strewn about the room. There was a very specific mystical routine that had to be strictly adhered to whenever entering his room, in order to insure that the monster would remain in his gloomy sanctuary and would not threaten the human occupants of the household. The sequence was particularly important at night, since as everyone knows, ghosts are nocturnal creatures.

Immediately upon entering his bedroom, our son had to peek inside his closet door to check that the ghoul was indeed in residence and not just wandering aimlessly about the room somewhere. An unexpected confrontation with this brain sucking banshee might cause him to emit his freezing vapors which would trap him until he chomped him to pieces with his foot long needle sharp teeth. The apparition might blow him out the window with his fetid breath, or he might just scare his pants off with his demoniacal roar. Although he had yet to be actually seen, this monster's countenance was well known. Under such perilous circumstances, the only prudent thing to do, was to check the closet first.

Once assured that the poltergeist was at his proper post, our son had to quickly slam the door shut, least the spook slip out. Continual eye contact with that closet door had to be maintained, as he proceeded to the sanctuary of his bed as quickly as humanly possible. This move in itself could prove extremely dangerous in our son's room, where a snowplow was often necessary to clear a path down the center of the room. However, Adam managed it by simply flying over the entire mess, and catapulting himself straight into bed, while simultaneously tearing at his top sheet and covers, in his frenzy to hide underneath. (In case of really hot weather, simply placing one's favorite stuffed animal over oneself also rendered a person completely invisible to the fiend).

To lie in the darkness without the established means of protection would be to invite disaster. The force of sheer willpower could hold the demon in the closet telepathically, unless someone inadvertently opened the closet door, and then the entire ritual had to be repeated before the creature got his hopes up about being set free.

I repeatedly reminded our son that his ghost was really not in his closet at all, but resided somewhere in the deepest recesses of his subconscious mind; in his Fright Lobe. Whereas his intelligent, rational brain knew that there was really no such thing as a resident phantom in his closet waiting to suck out his eyeballs, or a gooney in his toilet bowl wishing for the opportunity to bite him on the backside, his Fright Lobe is convincing him that there is a stronger possibility of this occurring than there is of his getting an "A" on his next spelling test. As an adult after all, I knew better than to believe that we had a hob-goblin haunting our home. Besides, this one was a pussycat next to the one that we had in our cellar when I was growing up.

CHAPTER 7

SOME FOOD FOR THOUGHT

I firmly believe that when it comes to appetites there are two distinctly different types of children in this world. One type eats to live, while the other lives to eat. We had them both. Adam doesn't have the time to digest a simple carbohydrate. He is in such a rush to get on with his life, he's been known to eat on the toilet so as to eliminate one extra step. There sits our son, Captain of the Commode, trousers dangling off one sneaker, devouring a peanut butter and jelly sandwich.

Food means absolutely nothing to this sort. At mealtimes they can become totally preoccupied with anything at the table other than food. They read everything on the packages out loud, so that chewing is out of the question. One time, in desperation, I removed all packages, bottles and boxes so that there were no labels of any sort to distract him. Only to hear him state with the absolute conviction of a politician:

"Mikasa fine china. Narumi, Japan. Fascination 5872."

Suddenly, it will dawn upon him that he has not done his homework, or made his bed (ever, I might add), or that he has not showered in three days. No secret there to the rest of us. The culinary sophistication of this type of specimen is limited. They will eat anything French-i.e: fries, toast, and Chef boy-R-Dee. Lavach however, is out.

"Dear, would you like to taste some of mommy's lavach?" I would ask sweetly.
"What? You want me to taste the wash?" Adam answers incredulously.

Besides Halloween candy, I couldn't imagine what our son existed on, except toothpaste. I know for a fact that this was a staple of his diet for years, as he averaged a giant size tube every two weeks or so. For a child who thought that brushing his teeth was a form of child abuse, this kid was quite a consumer. Interestingly enough, this was the child who could not get enough of his own toenails as a baby. I was never really sure if it was all a big show, or if he actually knew that there was no nutrition in a toenail. I would place a fresh bottle of milk in his playpen, which he would completely ignore. Instead, he managed to find a three-day-old one under the mattress and proceed to devour it as though it were the nectar of the gods. That would put him into a deep and satisfied sleep while I, aghast at my irresponsibility, would be frantically dialing poison control.

As our son began to crawl (it's amazing how fortifying curdled milk is), he graduated to the usual delicacies: prime pieces of wooly balls rolling around under the table, choice cuts of ants when he could catch them, an occasional loose fiber in the rug, and select pieces of jig saw puzzles. One time I nearly passed out at the color of what I found in his diaper. Only to be informed by his pediatrician that he most likely ate his orange and green crayons.

By the time he was old enough to speak, Adam was extremely suspicious of anything that might represent sustenance. Lunchtime went like this:

"What would you like for lunch today darling?" trying to sound very casual.

"Nothing", he would reply, sounding VERY casual.

"How about a sliced egg sandwich?" I inquire while bracing myself.

"OK, but no bread".

"A fresh hard boiled egg with salt then?" still enthusiastically.

"OK, but no egg."

As far as I could determine, Adam continued to exist on chewing gum and dirt until he was about seven years old. It seemed as though the more teeth he acquired, the less he used them. He became an embarrassment to us. In a Jewish-Italian household where most of us needed to go on a diet, he looked like a famine survivor.

Enter our British nanny, who liked to prepare such appealing dishes as "Shepherd's Pie", "Bubble and Squeak" and "Toad in the Hole". What child could resist such Sesame Street table d'hôte? Adam could. Together we schemed up what we referred to as our Play-Doh line: blue rice, lavender mashed potatoes, and red cream-of-wheat. Adults, by the way, have a difficult time swallowing any of this.

Ask Adam what he would like for a snack, and he would brighten up.

"Dog biscuits!" came the immediate reply. The dog loved it.

Another thing this kid was fond of is ice. I suspect that anything with no nutritional value known to man would do, but whenever the ice-cream truck would jingle outside, Adam would knock the door down in an attempt to be first in line.

On the other side of the flapjack, you have the type who is more concerned with eating than with breathing. Specifically our other three children. This, in spite of the fact that their idea of a well balanced diet is a bowl of popcorn on one knee, a brownie on the other and a bottle of diet soda in their hand. This repast is devoured while quoting the latest diet fad from their magazines.

I often sat in awe of their after school raid on the refrigerator which is accomplished with tactical and methodical precision. A blight of teenage locust attacks the wretched refrigerator, which cowers in the corner of the kitchen, prepared for the onslaught. The first things to go are anything that can be scarfed down instantly, followed by anything frozen but micro-wavable. Foods that require opening are overlooked, with the exception of ding-dong wrappers and soda cans, which can be ripped open simply by using ones teeth.

Nutritious foods are carefully avoided, along with uncooked foods or those located on the lower shelves or in dark corners, which is the "outback" of the ice-box. Eye-level foods are most vulnerable to attack, and above eye level go next. The defrosting and crisper draws are completely off limits for obvious reasons. One, they have to be opened, and two, they usually only contain cheap vegetables and other healthy foods.

This assault has a language all its own.
"There is nothing to eat in this house!" means that you are out of gummy anything.
"You are trying to starve me to death!" is the term used when the only food on hand requires preparation.
An "early dieter" is a person who diets early in the day, so that by three pm, anything goes (straight into their mouths).

I am still waiting for the day that scientists can genetically alter teenagers, allowing them to digest cellulose, like cattle. That way they could just go outside and graze on the lawn, instead of off our pantry shelves and out of our shopping bags. Saves mowing too.
"This needs salt" Adam says, standing in the light of the refrigerator door one early morning.
"What is it anyway?" he asks, holding up a slender whitish object.

"It's a glycerin fever suppository" I answer. "Try the one for nausea while you're at it"
No nutrition at all. It figures.

CHAPTER 8

THE LITTLE STARS IN MY EYES

I learned how to be a stage mother in Ohio when a friend of ours asked our first two girls to model some clothing for a buyer's magazine. Intuitive mother that I was, I saw this as the vehicle that would rocket the girls straight to stardom. That was about the only thing that I had in common with all the other mothers at the photo shoot. It's amazing how many people get Reynoldsburg, Ohio confused with Broadway.

The backstage of a photographer's session for a magazine layout is a zoo. The mothers are the animals. They would rip your heart out for a bobby pin. Touch one of their children's hairbrushes and you are dead meat. On the other hand, it's a great training ground for Black Friday shopping. Of course, everyone wants their child photographed first, before they get cranky for lunch, a nap or a cigarette.

Bonnie who was born in California, and considered membership in Actor's Equity her birthright, caught the acting bug during her debut as a grain of rice in the Thanksgiving Pageant. That was in elementary school. She went on to mesmerize the audience in The Wizard of Oz, in which she appeared as Oz Person #38. Pointing to the ceiling, she cringed in terror at the Wicked Witch's approach and screams "What's that!?" At this, the audience, which was made up entirely of the families of the actors feigned frozen panic or at least mild interest by the fifth performance or so. Of course her appearance in this spectacular required the services of a beautician, wardrobe mistress, and caterer. I was up to the task, and our star was launched.

I was more than interested therefore, when we got the phone call from a friend who was putting on a Christmas play at our church. She was in desperate straights when two of her "snow girls" blew off without notice to go on a ski vacation with their family. That's what you get for casting twins, I thought.

"Look, I know that this is kind of last minute, but I understand that Bonnie can sing and her sister can dance. Do you think that they could choreograph a quick dance to my music for our opening performance tomorrow night?" she pleaded. The number is called "Roly Poly Snowy Sort of Gals". Oh, and you'll need to make their costumes", she added as though it was an afterthought.

"Tomorrow night, huh?" While this might cause other moms to require smelling salts, to a stage mother, the smell of opportunity was enough.

"And for how large an audience?" I inquired, trying to seem nonchalant. "How many performances? Will it be aired on local TV?" "250-300 audience, three performances, cable TV and local newspapers" came the immediate response. I was beginning to salivate.

"OK", I agreed, "But only if Adam can be a reindeer". I'm a great agent. I really believed that our son had star quality too. Star quality being defined as "the ability to get on and off stage without wetting oneself". Adam got his horns.

Opening night is always exciting in live theater, as you never know what is going to happen. In children's theater, this applies to every other performance as well. You can count on it. What we didn't count on was rain. The kind of torrential rain that only happens in southern California, where it never rains unless it pours. As we floated into the church auditorium we couldn't help but notice that aside from the parents and siblings of the performers, the entire audience consisted of three elderly women who, stranded by the weather, were waiting for a ride home from the church's pot luck supper that night.

Undaunted by this, actually entirely oblivious of it, my friend (who was the writer, director, orchestra, etc.) appeared on stage at the appointed time to welcome the audience and explain the plot. A gripping tale of a little girl who about to find the true meaning of Christmas, aided by seven teddy bears, ten angels, a sprinkle of twinkling stars, a hand-full of snowflakes, six reindeer (formerly five) and two Roly Poly Sort of Girls!

Don't think that it escaped me for a minute that while I'd spent the past twenty-four hours riveting my fingers together with needles, thread and glue in order to turn two gangly little girls into cotton battened snow-girls, the star of the show appeared in her own nightgown. But I supposed one had to pay one's dues in this industry. And anyway, there was a camera man taping the show.

The curtain opened. In front of our eyes was a sight of sheer divinity. The diminutive stars twinkled in glittered tulle with matching satin ballet slippers. The tiny angels were swathed in pure white gauze; their pipe-cleaner halos bobbing up and down over their cherubic faces. The smiles on the snowflakes could melt the styrofoam snow scattered about and collected into authentic looking piles on the stage. Just as the music was about to flow from the keyboard, one of the twinkling stars tripped (over) the light fantastic, lost her footing and toppled into the first row of the audience. I ran for ice amid screams of panic.

The show went on, as all shows must. After briefing the cable TV camera man as to which parts my children were in, and spelling our name out for the newspaper reporter, I settled in next to my husband to enjoy the performance. Everything was going along quite well until halfway through the second act, when a tiny yelp was heard from the rear of the darkened audience. House lights went on immediately. There, lodged between a chair and the leg of a folding table left over from the pot-luck supper, was one of the snowflakes who never made it back to the stage from one of their escapades in the "scary forest".

The snowflake was restored to the stage, applauded on by an enthusiastic audience. The play continued until a fist fight broke out between two angels who had been having a noticeable difference of opinion regarding their "spot" ever since the beginning of the show. Each time they returned from the 'scary forest" both of them dashed for the spot closest to the Christmas tree. After some pushing and shoving, which cost one angel her wings, a teddy bear from the fourth grade broke it up. After a moment's hesitation, he tossed the broken wings into the first row of the audience, and took a bow.

It came time for my snow-girls to come on stage. I felt the familiar surge of adrenaline in my veins. I motioned to the TV cameraman who was busy wiping tears of hysterical laughter from his eyes while trying to regain his composure. My girls swept out on stage followed closely behind by a stagehand who had obviously not read the script, and who was trying desperately to shove them back behind the curtain. They made it to center stage before he did and began their routine. That's professionalism.

The play was in the final act. The reindeer, who quite audibly had been having a great time back stage for the past fifteen minutes or so, filed on stage. I counted five. I counted again. After a brief exchange of glances with my husband, I bolted backstage, only to find tiny Adam pinned behind the stage door. In their enthusiasm to get on stage, the taller reindeer had accidentally pushed him there. Huge tears of embarrassment, failure and abandonment welled up in his big soft brown eyes. A primitive maternal animal instinct took over. Somewhere between pity and rage, I popped the red nose on Adam and ushered him out on stage with Santa (our Deacon) to lead the others in the grand finale.

Everyone agreed that it was truly a night of the stars, a gala event. None of the little actors and actresses who were busy sucking on their candy canes even noticed the unimpressed audience as they headed out into the stormy parking lot. I couldn't wait to read the reviews.

CHAPTER 9

THE MOST IMPROVED MOTHER OF THE YEAR

The problem with teenage girls is that they never keep their opinions to themselves and they are always looking for ways to rearrange you. There is a secret competition among them to see who can improve their mother the most. The winner of this competition gets to be the undisputed fashion authority for the rest of the entire school year. Under these circumstances, my teens stand an excellent chance to win. The use of a comb would make a positive difference in me.

I wear socks with flip-flops in the winter. My outfits don't "come together". I'm lucky if they stay together while I am in them. I am not chic. What I know about fashion, you could write on the back of a barrette. I am completely unaffected by style, unaware of design, and often oblivious of size. I think functional. My heroines are the women who can wear polyester in 100-degree weather without melting into the carpeting. The girls have convinced each other that their real mother would never dress like I do.

"Wherever did you get those pants mom? They are totally generic and so outdated that I don't even know the name of that color!"

"Clearance rack, 1987. Bellbottoms are a real challenge to

shorten and I just got around to it. The color was called pumpkin".

My daughters on the other hand, have taken the simple task of getting dressed and turned it into a science. They quote fashion magazines by psalm and verse. They spend hours and small fortunes at the mall. Their labels have more to say then they do. They faint at the thought of a generic wristwatch. They can't go to the mailbox unless their hair has been tortured by the curling iron for an hour. I once threatened to have GUESS labels tattooed to their backsides so they would feel more confident entering a shower.

These are girls who know exactly which make-up brush to use for what, and how to use those packages of eye-shadow that contain seventy-five colors each. I, on the other hand, have been faithful to my navy blue eye shadow for the past twenty years and I haven't even used it up yet. They know the difference between a mudpack and molding mud. They faithfully follow a skin cleansing routine that would make Mary Kay choke up. Every Saturday morning they emerged from the bathroom looking like huge Smurfettes. Under their shower cap is a mixture that at one time was edible.

You can always locate the girls by following the sound of aerosol hairspray. One day, the older one emerged from the bathroom with a look of absolute horror on her face. Pointing to her once sable colored hair which now looked like it harbored an advanced case of head lice she screamed;

"Do you know what this is mom? This is hairspray buildup!"
Of course I knew what it was. I paid for it. And I knew perfectly well that I was about to invest in another product to eliminate it.

The fashion competition reaches full frenzy on Open School Night. The pressure of an erupting volcano is nothing next to the pressure these kids are under to turn out the perfectly coiffured mother. This is the fashion finals!

"Mom", the two older girls pleaded, "please WEAR something this year".

"And what did I do last year? Go naked?"

"For God sakes mom," one of them moaned. "Last year you wore white short shorts with green tights underneath! How déclassé!"

"It gets chilly at night this time of year" I protested.

"How about your hair mom". Her voice began to raise an octave. I grabbed my dishtowel to cover my burnt ends. Two weeks prior I had covered my gray roots with a frosting kit, then permed over it. I looked like a used Brillo pad.

"I'll just get it cut", I said "And I'm conditioning", I added miserably.

"You must stop OVERPROCESING!" she screamed. "Don't you know that you're dealing with living protein?"
Somehow I have a hard time thinking of my hair in terms of living. Existing maybe, but not actually breathing or anything like that.

"You know mom, you're not getting any younger. She was going to get nasty now.
"You really ought to come to the gym with us". Your ankles are getting as big as thighs."

"Those are my thighs. Things fall after four kids". The gym is a real sore spot with me. I knew I should have followed my intuition and invested in spandex years ago. Besides, the body that I want is not at the gym. It is on a 20 year old, Miss America hopeful.

"Your eyebrow pencil is too red. You really should try taupe".

"My brand only comes in light, medium and dark". I could hear myself starting to become defensive.

"What products do you use anyway?" they queried.

"For cooking or cleaning?"

"You know. To cleanse your face with".

"Soap and water. Oh, and a facecloth".

"That the very worst thing that you can use on your skin! They squealed in unison.

Don't you know ANYTHING about cleansing?", said the first.

" What's that perfume you are wearing? It smells strange", the other one asked suspiciously.

"It's disinfectant. I just scrubbed the bathrooms".
"Well then take a shower or something! You smell like a cleaning lady".

"I am the cleaning lady".

"And my life is in the toilet!" moaned the older one.

"I got an idea!" piped in the younger one. "Let's go shopping!"

I ask you. Where is Rumplestilskin when you need him? I look forward to going to the mall the way I look forward to termites in the attic. Besides that, their favorite store rivals any amuse-ment park for entertainment. The music registers 6.5 on the Richter scale. Lights are chasing each other around the ceiling like photons in heat.

The girls and I have two completely different shopping styles. They enter the store with the reverence and sanctity of a church. They ooze over to the closest rack of hot labels with an air of cool detachment and gaze pensively at the designs. I barge in and head directly for the clearance rack. While they slip over to the newest line of imported shoes, I am busy rifling through the table of marked down underpants. Waving a pair of acetate ones overhead like a flag I call out in the general direction of two mops of dark hair.
"Hey, didn't you complain that you needed new underwear?"

Dead silence. Even the music stopped. All heads turned in my direction. Eyes rolled in sockets. Telepathically the entire store of teenagers communicated with each other with these two words. "A parent". The back of some blonde head hissed at me.
"Don't EVER speak to me in PUBLIC".

"I'm not speaking to you", I replied politely. "I'm speaking to my daughter over there". My daughter was hiding behind a sweater with enough hair on it to require a collar and a license. It looked like it needed a bowl of water.

"Look" I continued. "You said that your underwear had just about HAD it, didn't you? So what about these?" I held up a pair of darling flowered bloomers that I had dug up from under a pile of garments that amounted to little more than a string and an eye patch.
"They're purple. I hate purple".

"No they're not. They're lavender. How about white?"

"White! I have a drawer full of white!"
"Pink then? Here's a pretty pair of pink bikinis".

"Pink is declasse".

"Red?"

"Red is a gang related color".

"Blue?"

"Their rival gang."

"Well, what color do you want then?" my voice rising danger-ously near the audible level again.

"I only wear white".

On open school night, when other moms showed up in silk dresses and pumps, I arrived attired in my children's clothing: mid-thigh jeans skirt, pullover top, slouchy socks and sneakers. My hair had been teased until it cried. Everything on me spoke designer. I was topped off with pearls everywhere; in my ears, in my hair, and on my blouse. I looked like a giant oyster had thrown up on me. My eyes, suffering from acid in the science lab began to tear, and my "waterproof" mascara chased one of my false eye-lashes down my cheeks and into my lap. I was beginning to look like a wax museum piece that was melting. The girls however, thought I looked stunning. They gave me a B+ that night. I think I made honor roll.

CHAPTER 10

THE GUILT LOBE

Somewhere, in that unwritten handbook that you get along with the baby, it clearly states that the human female brain weighs approximately 1/4 more than that of the human male. What accounts for such an appreciable difference is the evolution in the female of an additional sector of the brain. This sector is known as the Guilt Lobe.

The Guilt Lobe is the portion of the brain that demands that mothers accomplish the impossible. After a full week of working, cooking, cleaning and nurturing, mother might be tempted to collapse in a comma over the ironing board on Saturday. The Guilt Lobe is immediately alerted by this and insists that she gets right back up and take the dog to the vet for his shots. At the height of her malaise, there might be a temptation for mom to sneak a day off from routine; her feet propped up on the couch, feeling absolutely wretched from a bug. Her phone and her beeper will sound at that exact same moment . Some phone predator will be on the line while her husband is desperately trying to contact her regarding the dill pickle slices that are missing from his sack lunch. A fight-to-death argument erupts between two of the children over who currently has more scabs on their body. Just let mom's behind graze a couch pillow and watch all the electricity in the house go on strike, the toilet will throw up, and the dog will do the same on the couch. Why mothers were given backsides to begin with is a mystery. Everyone knows that they are only allowed to use them to push doors shut when their arms are full of groceries and babies.

In the laundry room, a troop of dirty clothes has embarked upon their own trek, storming their way out of the laundry chute, and proceeding to overtake and close off the only land access to the garage. Someone is already inquiring as to the status of their favorite shirt which has been missing in action since late yesterday when they stuffed it under a couch pillow for safe keeping while watching TV. It's astounding that out of twenty-seven shirts; this is only one that will "go" with black stone washed jeans. If that doesn't reduce you to a puddle of pity, add to this calamity the fact that the particular garment in question also happens to be their LUCKY shirt, without which this child will fail to make the cheer squad this year! This disaster will invariably lead to a total loss of popularity, and could result in the inevitable eating disorder, for which mom can take full blame.

It is the Guilt lobe that refuses to let our maternal identity die, or even rest. Every morning, sick or well, mothers drag themselves out of beds that they haven't yet slept in to fix their children a hearty breakfast before school. Any mother who fails to do so risks atonement for her sin by paying for the undernourished empty-head's education until the child is old enough to need bifocals to read the text books.

This sector of the brain feeds on the narcissistic attitudes of others. Faced with the fact that mom is still in the hospital on Wednesday, after having given birth on Monday, an incredulous wide-eyed look develops on the faces of her children. Who will drive them to soccer practice that afternoon? The Guilt Lobe thrives in an emotional Sahara such as this. Mom immediately dashes home from the hospital with presents for everyone. Under disbelieving eyes she proceeds to bake a cake and whip up a casserole for six from one hard-boiled egg, a leftover piece of cheeseburger, three strands of overcooked spaghetti and two packets of Chinese mustard. Good thing she caught the Gastro-Intelligent Gourmet on the TV in the labor room. The fact that she is the walking wounded does not register. The Guilt Lobe is running overtime, pointing out to her that resting is an indiscretion which will insure that her family will become exposed to an incurable illness stemming from the contagious life forms growing in glasses and dishes strewn throughout the house. Despite the fact that mom herself put every dish away in the cupboard after dinner, by the very next morning the dirty dish brigade is already lining up to begin the daily march across the kitchen counter, straight past the dishwasher, and on top of the refrigerator.

It is the Guilt Lobe that causes mothers to make apologies for visiting a beauty parlor instead of cleaning out the animal droppings from the flowerbeds. For going to the gym instead of disinfecting the toilet seat with a toothbrush. For taking a class in night school instead of reupholstering the dining room chairs, and for closing the door for some privacy when we use the bathroom. It is the guilt lobe that denies us the right to our own dry toothbrush, a pair of eyebrow tweezers that don't have to go in for realignment before they can be used, or a hairbrush that didn't grow a fur coat since the last time we saw it. We apologize for everything from our husband's un-groomed ear and nasal hairs to our children's metabolic disorders. And it is the Guilt Lobe that is responsible for our stubbornly and uncompromisingly high standards and our neurotic aspirations to maternal perfection.

What ever happened to the TV moms that we were brought up on? The ones, who are always seen floating on clouds of pillows, drifting in a sea of fresh cut flowers, or melting at the taste of divine chocolates? The memory alone is enough to make you want to go out and borrow a disease. But then, I look at my beloved offspring, and the Guilt Lobe goes into time and a half. Surely I couldn't be as ill as my ten year old son who drags himself to the breakfast table looking as though he'd spent the entire night up in a laboratory somewhere inventing his dreams. Nor could my suffering ever reach the proportions of my fourteen year old daughter who actually did spend the night up, totally despondent over the loss of a finger nail.

I'm not sure if this type of masochism is actually terminal, but I'm willing to bet that a good number of us would die of shock if we were allowed one whole day in bed to be sick. And so, we moms pump water down ourselves until we leak, and overdose on iron supplements until we rust. The fact that the Guilt Lobe resides somewhere in our subconscious, is something that we find hard to get into our heads. Sadly, there is no way for us to deal with our Guilt Lobe through analysis. The key to our survival calls for, at the very least, a complete psychological transplant.

CHAPTER 11

GROWING PAINS

I'm sure that I do not risk being mistaken for Dr. Spock on this, but I have been noticing distinct changes in our four children's senses over the years. For instance, it has been my experience that children go deaf around the age of two, and do not regain this ability until they begin to notice the opposite sex. No matter how many times you tell them to do their homework or be in before dark, they will swear on a stack of baseball cards that they never heard such a thing.

This loss of hearing is completely restored at puberty, when all they have to do is look at you to hear what you are thinking about them. At this developmental stage, any secret that you might whisper inaudibly to your spouse is in danger of becoming public knowledge among their friends. The fact that this hearing is selective, is painfully evident in the volume of their music, which threatens to return them and you, to the previous state of deafness.

The sense of smell is greatly inhibited during the elementary school years. No matter how radioactive their feet might be, children never seem cognitive of the fact that they stink. After several days of observing the same outfit on our son, I have to peel it off of him and purge it. Forcing a child to brush their teeth is viewed as child abuse. The act of passing intestinal gas is perfected and glorified.

Judging by popular confectioneries and cold cereals, many children suffer an accompanying loss of taste as well. Others become "picky eaters". They will examine food, dissect it, and lean over it and spit in it. They will stare it down, make ugly faces at it, cry over it, or ignore it completely. They will invent ingenious methods to dispose of it, such as stuffing it down the baby's diaper, or squirrel it away in their cheeks or napkins. The only thing that they won't do with it, is eat it.

Again, the sense of taste makes a reappearance during the teenage years when, in a matter of mere seconds, a couple of hungry youths can clean out your refrigerator down to the light bulb, strip the pantry down to the roach motel and begin ruminating through the grocery bags. This interest in food will persist into old age, alternating spurts of burning culinary curiosity, with bouts of heartburn and gout.

The loss of vision, as evidenced by the appearance of any teenager's room, is quite sadly, only restored in the female. In the male, this adolescent phenomenon is carried into adulthood, rendering him completely incapable of finding anything on his own. At home, he will act as a houseguest. "Where do we keep the toilet tissue?" he will ask for the third time in one week. "Are my slippers under the couch?" This leads to the necessity of his finding a mate, upon whom he can blame his blindness. "Who took my keys", he will roar." staring directly at them. "I know I put my glasses in this exact spot!" he will convince only himself. "Someone must have moved the freeway entrance again!" he will announce in the wrong town.

The female, on the other hand, will hone the sense of vision to a fine point. By the time she is middle age, she will detect each and every microscopic line on her face. She will be able to see dirty ears on her children who have not yet emerged from the shower. She will notice dust on her daughter's coffee table from a photograph. She can see any trouble that might involve her family coming, a mile away.

The final insult to the human spirit of course, is the deterioration of the memory, which all children suffer. Inquire as to his whereabouts all day, and your son will develop a glazed look, such as to give a parent causes to check his ability to dilate properly. Probe further and he will become completely catatonic. Do not let this throw you. These children possess selective memory. While they are hard pressed to remember what they learned in algebra that very afternoon, or who the current U.S President might be, they can faithfully recite every word of every rap song that they ever heard on the radio.

And although my eyes are competing with my mind to see which can expire first, I have decided that growing old is not so bad after all. All I have to do is to learn how to cope with these poor old physically frail, slightly menopausal youngsters that I live with.

CHAPTER 12

IT TAKES A STRONG CONSTITUTION

Yesterday I gave final rites to our two older daughter's bedrooms. The poor things never had a chance. As I cautiously opened the door to "D" room a crack, I saw a sight that no mother should have to witness. As usual, all the drawers were wide open, and all of her clothes had escaped. I actually caught a pair of pantyhose in the act of slithering out of the top drawer. Two wet towels were huddled pathetically in the corner, freezing to death. Several tissues were in stages of deterioration on her night table, and a sock was molting under her makeup vanity. The smell began to make my toes curl.

I peeked into "C" room. The garbage pail, in which she stores her history notes, was regurgitating its contents back onto the floor. Limp jogging pants, smelling quite alive, were exhaustedly draped over dirty clothes piled high enough to cover the wall in which I was sure that we had installed a window when we built the house. Something once drinkable had solidified in a cup, and a nail file was riveted into the center of it. From under a blouse, a single sad sneaker peered out, searching for its significant other. Under her bed, you could find the lost continent.

The biggest pigs in the world do not live in the circus sideshow, nor do they compete at the county fair. They are not listed in the Guinness Book of Records. They are living right here in this house. Grease stains monogram their T-shirts and their sheets are identifiable by the dried-on nail polish. If they ever did their laundry, they could triple the value of stocks in companies manufacturing laundry spray .They have made it necessary for us to increase our home insurance policy to cover individuals who would enter their rooms. I don't know how they can find anything or anyone in there without radar. It remains a medical enigma that girls who can jump twice their height to do a "lay up" for a basketball team, or a get "put up" for a cheerleading team, are too arthritic to bend over to pick up their underwear. On the other hand, if they ever decided to hang all of their clothes, they could cause a severe hanger shortage.

Over in the corner, trying to look inconspicuous as possible, was something large and square with doodles all over it. I couldn't resist the temptation to find out what it was, until I realized that it was her algebra book! Something in my mind suddenly snapped. I asked myself. "Must we mothers blame ourselves if our teenagers rooms look like a high-school locker room after a Friday night game?" "Of course!" came the reply. After all, the only thing I ever trained our children to pick up was take out. They are slobs, and they are good at it. Besides, these were not first generation slobs, I had to remind myself. They had inherited the gift from their parents, and had merely improved upon it.

I have come to believe that your body is the temple of your soul, and your room is the sanctuary of your mind. The least I could do was to say a prayer before I lost mine.

CHAPTERS 13

READ IT AND WEEP

I t dawned on me one day that the only literature that I ever saw the kids studying were magazines. These are children who regularly slip their class notes under their pillows at night, in the sincere belief that the Brain Fairy will come and help them to absorb facts through their pillowcases. They use books for much more utilitarian purposes: for propping up a mirror so that they can apply their makeup, or to stack up instant additional seating, or as a door stop. When they were younger, they used to line up all their books across the floor, creating a "bridge" over an imaginary bed of smoldering molten lava. The idea that books can be stepping stones to a successful future never enters their mind.

The Duchess of Disorder, has as hard a time keeping her thoughts straightened out, as she does her room. There were times that I would have liked to give her brain a good airing out. Like the time that she had to write a report on St. Thomas, the disciple of Christ for her religion class.

"Did you do your report on St. Thomas yet?" I asked, a full week before it was due. I always like to begin this line of questioning a week early, so as to give the kids a jump start on there excuses.

"Yep, all finished", came the confident reply.

"Really? What did you learn?" I asked sweetly.

"Let's see. He was born in England 1227.

"St Thomas the disciple?!" I asked suspiciously. "Isn't that a bit late to be walking with Jesus? Especially considering that He died in AD 33?"

"This is religion mom," she began patiently, "You just gotta have faith".

"I have faith. I just don't believe that he could have been born in England. "Jesus wasn't British you know" I countered. "Wait a minute, could you be talking about St. Thomas Aquinas"?

"Yeah! That's the one!"

"Honey, that's the wrong saint!" I moaned.

"So, what's your point ma?" And to think, when she was born all she had confused were her days and nights.

"You wrote your report on the wrong man. That's my point!"

"So? Can I use it or not? I mean, they were both saints, weren't they?"

"Of course you can't use it! Your teacher wants a report on the disciple." I replied, trying to keep my voice from going up an octave. Her squinted eyes told me two things. First, she was lucid. Secondly, she was beginning to get the picture.

"You mean that I have to do this ENTIRE report all OVER again?" she squealed.

I asked myself. Could this be the same child that knows every brand of hair preparations by heart? She was in danger of floating away! Like a hot air balloon! I began to get the idea that I'd better look into the business of our children's education a little more closely. This is actually a lot less scary than looking into their backpacks. There, all you will see is crumpled up tissues, half eaten candy bars, and some old notes that were passed in class. It seemed appropriate to ask her where her books were.

"What books?" she asked as though she had just joined the world. "What do you mean, what books? Textbooks! What are they preparing you to become anyway an expert in unemployment? Math books! History books! Science books!" I saw that I was going to have to slow down here, so as not to lose her completely.

"Oh, those" she replied with a glimmering of understanding. "We don't get them any more in most subjects. Unless we check them out of the library."

"That's absolutely pathetic!" I shrieked.

"What?"

"Pathetic- from the Greek word Pathos. Go look it up in the dictionary. It's that big black book that your using as a TV tray."

It frightens a parent at first to realize that the schools are no longer providing books for students to take home. When we went to school it was understood that the heavier you schoolbag, the better a student you were. Intelligence was measured in pounds per square foot. It was drilled into our heads that books shed light upon our environment, illuminating our path to understanding. The heavier the books, the brighter the beacon. These kids were just not pulling enough weight around. I was about to make a call to the school to see about getting some reading materials issued, when suddenly it dawned upon me. On the one hand, the possibility exists that without books, our children might have to stay in college until all the jobs are gone. On the other hand, there exists and even stronger possibility that the books would just be used as bedroom furniture anyway.

CHAPTER 14

THE DEMON OF THE DUST

What happens to a man's mind when he is transported from his normal ineffectual, mundane work day existence, and is suddenly endowed with limitless power? Let's take for instance, any kind, loyal, honest, modest individual, and elevate him to the exalted status of "Referee", and just watch a metamorphosis occur that would make a werewolf cringe.

Suddenly, this little man becomes the absolute authority on everything concerning the sport, regardless of whether or not he is even capable of understanding a play. He is the judge. He is to be treated with absolute reverence, and his authority, unlike his character, is unquestionable. After all, his decision is final! You can't get more omnipotent than that, can you?

Unlike his fellow monsters, this incubus is not invoked by the full moon. It is the rising of the Saturday morning sun that induces his supernatural materialization. A maniacal gleam appears in his sepia colored squinted little eyes, as he mulls over how many unpopular calls he might achieve in a one-hour game. His entire countenance takes on a demoniacal demeanor as he contemplates how many coaches he can chew up, and how many players he can digest. As he dons his cleats, he actually gains stature. His beard sprouts, his canines erupt; the muscles in his miniscule brain begin to bulge, erasing any trace of humanity that might have existed.

Armed with a Styrofoam cup of coffee and a jelly donut, he approaches the field with an air of cold determination. There is hush over the crowd as he makes his grand entrance onto the grass. The five and six year old players immediately stop pushing each other and picking their noses and assemble for opening play. As the silence reaches a deafening crescendo, the "ref" nods his head. The lions are released from their cages, and thumbs begin to rise.

The ritual never fails to amaze me, as I sit huddled under my umbrella wearing three layers of clothing to watch our first game of the day. With four children on three different teams, I will "peel down" to my underwear by the third game, when the temperature reaches nearly one hundred degrees at 4 p.m. Through an established Morse Code of glances and winks, the coaches confer with each other across the field, with regards to the "ref's" reputation. The broadcast reads; "this one is tough", "this one is unreasonable", or "this one is a raving lunatic". I have witnessed parents of wealth, social status and even of athletic renown brought to their knees by this creature, as they made the unforgivable error of questioning one of his calls.

Suddenly, a shrill whistle halts the play. As confusion gives way to undivided attention, the referee's hand shoots up into the air and points downward at the accused (who is clearly a whole foot taller than himself).

"Red card! Red card, Red card!" he shouts at the top of his lungs. My word, I think, is he really going to give out three red cards to one individual?

"Do you question my authority?!" he screams imposingly at the condemned criminal. Actually I think it's his ability to read the rulebook that is in question.

All eyes turn to the ostracized individual, who immediately assumes the glazed appearance of an ashtray in a ceramics oven. He slinks off the field in shame and disgrace, mindful of the symbol of his indiscretion, that burns acridly in his hand.

As the game ends, His Royal Heinous stomps off the field, confident that he had displayed immense superiority and wielded enormous power over his subjects. In complete control of every situation, he hunts for his car that he lost in the parking lot which also contains his keys. In command of every move, he wipes the jelly stain off the coveted shirt that made him what he was for one whole hour that Saturday.

CHAPTER 15

CAMP COMMOTION

It came to pass, that one day the man did take it upon himself to make The Plan for the next family vacation. And so it was that he booked them into the Camp Garden of Eden for a solid week, only to discover that the Assumptions were incorrect and the camp was indeedth a nudist colony. And darkness was upon the face of the woman. And the man and the woman fought among themselves on the matter. And she spoke unto him saying:
"You are indeed small of brain that none may profit from your choices."
And he answered unto her:
"And you are surely big of mouth that none may abide by your comments!"

And so the woman looked down upon the man as the camel that doth spit in the eye of his master. Then, the children that sprang forth from this union spoke unto the man and the woman and said to them:
"Why doth thou argue this matter when thou mayest vacation without ever leaving thy tent?"

And the man and the woman both looked upon these offspring that they had begotten as though they were several grains short of a desert. Yet, in their wisdom they harkened upon this New Plan, and they saw that indeed it was also good. And that's how the idea of vacationing at home happened!

In the beginning of the summer we had four children. By the end of August, with temperatures outside of over one hundred degrees, there were at least three hundred of them inside. Children's faces came and went. Sometimes they were ours. I organized, soothed, refereed, comforted, reprimanded, fed, watered and dispensed both crayons and first aid as befitted the disaster.

Kids came over to our house to sleep dragging their pillows and teddy bears. They went home leaving behind pillows, teddy bears, slippers and underwear. My home became an orphanage for homeless bathing suits, a half-way house for single roller skates.

Occasionally our children chose to sleep over at a friend's house. Mysteriously, by mid-summer there wasn't a dark haired child in our house, although all four of ours have brown hair. One day in August I triumphantly announced to my husband that I had potty trained the baby. He pointed out (very gently due to my delicate state of mind), that our youngest child was in fourth grade.

No one could agree upon what to do at any given time. One wanted to nap in the same room that three others chose to rap. The TV, tape player and computer games competed with each other hour after hour, day after day, while hundreds of dollars of toys gathered dust on the shelves. Our son sat for hours trying to communicate telepathically with the dog. Then he found some toothpicks and glue and went into construction. My best poker deck was used to build a castle, and several cards ended up with little square holes cut out of them for windows.

One day, I lost my head completely, pulled out all the plugs and insisted that the kids find a game to play. There they sat, bored, mopey and slightly comatose, until one of them discovered the cartons from my new washer and dryer on the driveway and turned them into a fort. As home improvements go, these had to be the best investments we ever made.

Inside, our home looked like a haunted house. Sheets and covers were strewn across all the couches and chairs. Underneath them, children and animals were camped out sharing their food. Take it from someone who has lived with babies under her blouses for six years straight. Kids don't know the difference between a tuna casserole and dog food. Dogs do.

The police stopped over when the noise level registered eight on the Richter scale. Morbid curiosity had caused a neighbor to actually record what they heard going on in our house. I was impressed by the results. The garage door slammed 42 times. The front doors beat out the garage door by a slight margin, despite the fact that no one ever left. The rear doors swung in at over 60 due to the presence of the pool, and were topped only by the refrigerator. This is perfectly understandable, in the light of the fact that our son uses the refrigerator as his personal air conditioner. Bathroom doors out slammed bedroom doors at 54, and car doors really trailed. But only because there were only two drivers in the house. They really deserved a handicap.

Finally, the microwave door broke down under the stress. That same day the dog developed a nerve rash and had to go on sedatives. In desperate need of a full night's sleep, we threw the kids out to sleep under the stars. And that's how the idea of camping out in tents came about!

After a full school schedule of dances, roller skate nights, bowl-a-thons, awards assemblies, school plays and field trips, it's understandable that kids need a summer break from their grueling educational routines. I however, would rather fight a serious case of roach infestation.

CHAPTER 16

COOPED UP IN A COUP

I'm still not convinced that it is all that necessary to wake four sleepy children out of their needed rest in the middle of the night in order to go somewhere to relax. What is even more suspicious, is how my husband always managed to outnumber the other five of us whenever we voted on the issue. And as usual, I'd find myself dragging four zombies out in the dark to the back of the station wagon, which we had prepared like a hospital ward the night before. Handling them as one would hollowed out Easter egg shells, I'd reposition them on their pillows in the car. Looking forward to some quiet road time before the morning rush hour, my husband and I would speak in hushed whispers. This usually lasted until we got on the freeway entrance ramp, when a head would pop up from the back.

"Mom, I forgot to go to the bathroom."

These are the dreaded words of the road. Immediately, I would throw an accusing glance at my husband who had no inclination what-so-ever of giving up his spot in the fast lane for his own child. Men never seem to get it. It's a medical phenomenon that the same man who is always in the bathroom when you need him, never feels the urge to stop on the road. Suddenly their bladders become the size of beach balls. They store their water indefinitely in their egos. They just sit there behind the wheel, maintaining themselves in a state of suspension like a viral spore.

Mothers, on the other hand, having suffered psychologically from the trauma associated with their children's potty training, would stop the car in the middle of a bridge if necessary, to let children out to relieve themselves.
"I think there's an all night diner up ahead", he states in an all too nonchalant manner.
"How FAR ahead?", I counter suspiciously.
"Oh, just five minutes or so".
"FIVE MINUTES?!!!! You expect this poor child to suffer for a full five minutes while you sit there and enjoy the scenery?"
"For crying out loud Susan, she's fourteen years old!".

What I am really savvy about when it comes to these family "bonding type" trips, is that the oil cartel has figured out the exact week when the greatest number of families will go globe-trotting around their own country. That's the week that gasoline prices go up faster than the tally at the grocery checkout counter. Gas stations actually have to hire an extra attendant just to change the gasoline price signs hourly. And aren't we all just sick to death of the same old excuses:

- "Sealed barrels of oil have dried up as a result of a two thousand year old curse in the Middle East"
- "A fossil fuel eating dinosaur has been spotted off the coast of Canada and has eaten all the shiploads of crude oil headed for the United States."
- " Natural gas is a rare commodity (around whose house?) and is being used faster than it is being produced!"

It doesn't matter that we have to take out a second mortgage on our house to afford these trips. Or that our past family automobile trips make Chevy Chase's vacation look like a trip to Disneyland. My husband and I are a determined if slightly demented team, devoted to our family's pleasure of the road. We plan well in advance. We take blankets and pillows to suffocate the troublemakers. We take games with over 1,000 pieces, in order to keep the kids busy picking them out of the crevices of the car seats. Reading material is used for little else than propping little ones up on, so that they can see out of the windows before they throw up. Then there's the cooler chest full of healthy snacks and drinks, which I always end up trying to eat all by myself while the kids stop at every candy store and fast food restaurant along the route.

It's no wonder that I gain fifteen pounds on vacation. Every time a child adds another doggy bag from their last restaurant meal to the cooler, I automatically start to calculate which was the oldest, and plan it for my next snack. My kids have never even heard of cold bread, no less cold leftovers. Never the less, the minute we hit our destination for the day, the kids practically kill each other trying to get to the ice machine. The hero is the one who dumps fresh ice on the sour milk and black bananas in the cooler. Another thing I will never understand, is why a candy bar bought in another state should taste any different from the one bought at our local market. The little ones however, who are on some kind of fact finding tour for the Congressional Confectionery Committee, insist on buying their favorites in every town that we pass through.

By the time that we get half way to our final destination, I'm ready to hop a flight home. I've heard "I'm telling" and "I'm gonna kill you!" and "ouch" more times than I can count. I have lost dental fillings from the volume of the music blasting from their headphones. It's no wonder that they're too deaf to hear me yell at them to lower it.

There is a certain reassurance however in the fact that we expect all of this on any given trip. It's like visiting an old vacation spot that we have come to know over the years. There is comfort in routine. As a matter of fact, there is a play that we reenact over and over on every trip. No one here needs a script any more, so I saved this one for you.

LONG DAY'S JOURNEY INTO INSANITY

As the curtain opens we see six people in a Ford Country Squire station wagon, baggage strapped to the top. There are two parents in the front seat, with an eleven-year-old son between them. In the back seat are two female teenagers with a greenish looking nine-year-old girl in between them. The road sign reads "Welcome to Pittstop, AZ. Please check all fresh fruit and children for bug infestation".

Nine year old: "How much longer?"
Mother (annoyed): "I just answered that question not five minutes ago. Why do you keep asking?"
Nine year old: "No reason. Only, how old do you have to be before you stop barfing in the car?"
Mother (whipping into wild animation): "Stop the car immediately!"
Father (in a bored tone): " I guess I could use some gas."
Mother (mumbling to herself): "Obviously he can't smell any better than he can hear".
Father: "Does anyone here need to use the restroom?"
Nine year old (as she races out of the car and makes a bee line for the lady's room): "I do!"
(There is a slight pause, as father begins to fuel up and the nine year old disappears out of sight).
Second Teenager: "She is such a brat. Why does she always have to go to the bathroom?"
Mother: "Because her bladder is smaller than yours, as is her mouth."
Second Teenager: "Oh, SURE. She just wants to do everything. I'll bet she gets something while she's in there. She's so selfish!"
(At this point the nine year old emerges from the store with a cold

drink in one hand and a beef jerky in the other hand).
First teenager (pops her head up and stares irately at the nine year old who is emerging from the store): "Jeeze! Look what she got!"

Mother (innocently, as though she hadn't heard that last remark): "Would anyone like anything from the store? I would be glad to give you all some money to buy yourselves something".
Son (enthusiastically): "You bet mom! I'd love some. Thanks!"
(Mother shells some cash out to the son, and he skips off whistling, while the other two girls sink down further in their seats and cross their arms in a pout).
First Teenager: (self righteously): "Absolutely not! And SHE didn't need anything either. I just KNEW that she didn't have to barf! She's so spoiled!"
Second Teenager: "She's so selfish, she has to have everything. (Turning to the nine year old in question who is approaching the car). "YOU just HAD to have that beef jerky didn't you? Now how do you expect mom and dad to afford the hotel room?"
First Teenager: "When I was your age, we weren't allowed to have beef jerky. All we got was beef!"
Nine year old: "Shut up both of you before I rip the pupils out of your eyeballs!" (She gets back into the car).
First Teenager: "Jerk".
Second Teenager: "You're such a stuck up little creep!"
(As the father gets back into the car, a chorus is sung by the teenagers, and joined by the son).
"Selfish, selfish, you're so selfish".
(This chorus can be repeated until the mother goes berserk or, at the director's discretion, he may have the mother whip around and whack the first kid available. It doesn't really matter which child she smacks. If this argument wasn't their fault, they surely did something else.)

While it's no picnic to start a vacation like this, it's almost impossible to be a happy camper once you arrive at your destination. The teenagers of course, have had their "one hour to landing" notice and have spent that time piling on makeup, popping zits, and asphyxiating the rest of us with hairspray, deodorant and perfume. We are a rolling fire hazard as we approach the motel parking lot. That is assuming that we do in fact reach our proper destination. On one trip we passed through the same town in Texas four times in two days; disproving once and for all that "all roads lead to Rome". After that I took a self-defense course in map reading.

The little ones enter the hotel lobby with yellow teeth, matted hair, wearing each other's clothing and looking like a chorus line from "Annie". The other guests stare at you trying to see some family resemblance, or to see if they can recognize any of the kids from pictures on milk cartons or on flyers

Whoever said that "getting there is half the fun", must have been talking about either getting inebriated or having an orgasm.

CHAPTER 17

IF THIS IS MY BREAK, WHY AM I CRACKING UP?

Vacation is defined as "a period of rest and freedom from work or study; a time of recreation." To full-time mothers, this should mean a break from shopping, and housekeeping. Compare this to reality.

Despite all odds, we arrive at our vacation destination. and I hit the first supermarket I see for tanning oils and enough snacks and drinks to feed a small but starving nation, along with enough plastic cups, bowls and utensils to cater an informal wedding. I also unpack those that I have saved along the way, wash them in the tiny sink in the bar, and carefully lay them out on my facial towel.

By day two there is a trail of plastic-ware, from the sink to the front door and I am starting to miss my dishwasher. I am back to the supermarket for sunburn preparations, blow-up pool toys, and beach towels.

By day three, I am browsing the newspapers for a sale on sandals or flip flops that someone forgot to pack.

By day four, I am back at the local mall with four kids firmly in tow, trying to ward off our teenagers' mall with-drawl symp-toms. No matter; we needed to pick up an emergency prescrip-tion for swimmer's ear at the pharmacy anyway.

I've hung wet towels and bathing suits over balconies by day, and with the exception of one half of a bathing suit that had dis-appeared, folded them and put them back in the proper drawers after supper. By noon on day four I have found the guest laundry, and I'm on my second load. I try not to think about my mother's portable iron that I refused to pack. I'm afraid to let housekeep-ing in without an accident policy, and I'm tired of having to help them find the beds. So I change the sheets myself and leave them outside the door along with the used towels and the trays that my husband and I brought up to the sleeping kids before the hotel stopped serving breakfast.

While the kids are at the pool, I again fold all the clothes strewn about the rooms, pick up crayons and coloring books, retrieve sunglasses lost under couch pillows, return rented VCR's to the desk and check the "stock" in the refrigerator and cooler chest. I stop by the pool on my way to the supermarket, just to make sure that everyone is enjoying themselves, and to reassure them that I will be back before lunch to mediate differences of opinions on restaurants.
"Where do you want to go to eat?", I ask upon my return.
"Burger Queen!", says the youngest.
"But you can get that at home", I patiently explain. "How about a little local flavor?"
"But I like the flavor of their crumpled up French fries", she moans.
"How about the Chinese restaurant next to the hotel?" I inquire hopefully.
"Do they have French fries?" she asks.
"They're Chinese, not French, you jerk!" sneers teenager number one.
"Hey! I feel like a bunch of ribs", pipes in the son.
"You are a bunch of ribs", says teenager two. "I got it! Lets order

pizza in with a movie!"

"But, you can get that at home!" I blurt out. How about a little local........." oh, what's the sense. Apparently I am too dumb to know that I was outnumbered before I began.

By the last day of our vacation some of us are in a state of complete relaxation, while others are in a state of total collapse. I look out of the window from the guest laundry room. Our oldest daughter is floating like a bubble on top of the water, sunglasses on, hair spread around her head like Medusa. The second teenager is also floating from the side of the pool, anchoring herself to the concrete edge by her legs. She is sipping a diet soda through a straw. I make a mental note that it was the last one in the cooler chest. The little ones, now the color of a crayon, were floating serenely by, eyes closed, and heads devoid of thought. Together they created a huge air pocket on the water.

I was exhausted. I hadn't slept well since we left home due to my husband's snoring. I refused the earplugs that he so graciously brought along for me. Why should my ears be put into solitary confinement, I reasoned, when it's his nose that was making all the trouble? I began to plan the car ride home. I looked forward to this the way I looked forward to another gray hair.

Then something snapped inside my head. "That's it!" I thought. "I'm going to sit down on a lounging chair and read." I grabbed the novel that I started when our oldest began teething, marched past our second child who was sprawled out on a lawn chair, hooked up to her ultrasonic umbilical cord, mumbling mindless phrases to the grass. The other one sat basted in sunscreen, peering into a magnifying mirror practicing self-mutilation on an ear lobe in order to accommodate a second earring in it.

"Are you going shopping?" she jumped up excitedly. "Don't forget the list! I need baby oil, lip balm, and a fashion magazine."
"Forget it" I snapped.

"Gosh mom, you're really stressing", said the first. "It must be PMS."

What did we mothers ever do before PMS? The only thing that prevented me from giving her a piece of my mind right then and there, was the nagging suspicion that I had none left to spare.
"And you", I turned to the second one, "Why can't you memorize your science like you memorize that drivel?"

"Gee mom", comes the indignant retort, we need SOMETHING to take our minds off thinking!" If they thought any less they would be legally brain dead. I pulled my son to my side lovingly.
"What a great opportunity to bond with our son!", I exclaimed to my husband who was busy examining the cooler chest for the absentee diet sodas.

"Sure" he commented sarcastically.
He had observed the routine one time too many to believe that I would let any opportunity slip by to perform my motherly duties. I didn't fool him for a minute. As I looked deeply into our son's huge brown eyes, I checked to see if there were any circles around them to indicate either a lack of sleep or a vitamin deficiency. Softly, I caress his sweet cheek, simultaneously noting any signs of fever. Gently, I smoothed down his cowlick, peeking around his temples for any signs of head lice. Playfully, I wrinkled up my nose and nuzzled his, searching for the minty flavor of toothpaste. Finally I nipped him on his left ear, peering inside to see if it accidentally got washed in the shower.

"Did he pass inspection?" asked my husband with his eyes on the last apple we had packed.
Suddenly, before I could answer, from our room we heard a blood-curdling scream emanating from our room. "HELP! I'M DYING!"
I set a new world record sprinting up the stairs almost killing myself in the process, only to find our youngest child glued to the TV screen playing Nintendo.

"Phew, that was a close one!" she said as she looked straight into my open jaw. "Hey mom, got any more whipped cream for the strawberries?"

"No! And don't you think that dad and I deserve a vacation too?" Dead silence followed, as she inspected me in her vague hypnotic way.

"It's a simple YES or NO answer, not an essay question!" I shouted. "What's the matter with your kids anyway?" I asked my husband as I rejoined him at the pool.

"They're spoiled", he said. "As in the context of rotten"

But memories fade, and we only remember what we care to. I remember the essay our son wrote when he returned to school:

MY VACATION

This was the best vacation I ever had! I spit at my big sister seven times and only got caught twice. I ate candy for breakfast and didn't take a bath the whole time. I swallowed a dime, and got it back the very next day. Our molly had babies while we were gone and we got to keep the ones that she didn't eat. But the very best part of it all was when we left my little sister in the bathroom at the truck stop and didn't remember her for almost a whole hour! Mom gave dad "time out" for a week!

I can always catch up on my rest in fifteen years or so.

CHAPTER 18

A FOOL AND HIS RULE

It seems like child psychologists are forever coming up with a better formula for raising well prepared, mentally balanced, healthy children; while we mothers cannot be trusted with the recipe for bathwater. Furthermore, they are continually prepared to share their profound twaddle with us, and if you don't subscribe to any of the magazines or read any books written on the subject, don't panic. You will eventually be informed through memos sent home from school.

One such piece of luminary literature that our son brought home from elementary school stated, "Children who are continually urged into accomplishing what should be automatic routine, will never learn to become independent". Hosanna! It further encourages mothers to leave these children to suffer the consequences of their own actions (or in this case, the lack of them). They assure us that "This course of events will result in a positive learning experience for the mother". I rate the reality of this piece of luminary literature right up there with Jack And The Beanstalk.

Do these people know what they are asking for? Do they really picture mothers luxuriating in bed on a school morning while their catatonic youngsters whip around the kitchen preparing themselves a hearty breakfast? Do they see us sipping a leisurely second cup of coffee as we watch these empty heads expertly zipping through their toiletries? Do their visions include us phoning up a friend for breakfast while our children automatically scramble around gathering books and school supplies from every corner of the house, and madly dash out the door to meet the school bus on time?

Maybe it's just us. Our nine-year-old son cannot read and chew at the same time. This morning he is reading. I implore him to finish breakfast and chase him off to brush his teeth. He walks off with a blank look on his face and immediately proceeds to settle himself on the bathroom floor to admire the dust particles floating around in a shaft of sunlight. I holler in to inquire as to his progress, jolting him back to reality for a fraction of a second. Off again, like a light wave, he begins to draw a cartoon in toothpaste on the sink top. This one depicts his tooth running away from decay germs. When he doesn't appear after fifteen minutes, I charge after him, only to find him absorbed in the complexities of the screw cap on the tube of toothpaste.

"So, when is the last time that you brushed your teeth?", I inquire, inspecting the mildew growing on his canines.
"Just before!", comes the indignant reply.
"Before what? Bedtime?, Christmas? Kindergarten?!"

I would very much like the opportunity to write a reply to this memo that our son brought home from school. Just to clarify a few elementary points which the learned PhD seems to have missed. My memo would read like this:

To Whom It Better Concern,
The following information is based upon data gathered in the field and compiled by mothers and other caretakers of young elementary school boys. The conclusions are based upon our collective observations and all facts are accurate and verifiable. Just

ask me.

Boys can go to school every day in the same outfit, unless a stronger force grabs them and peels it off. The very next day they will go looking for the same outfit which by then of course, is in the wash. Having exhausted that option, they will happily go nude.

Little boys are collectively known as The Great Unwashed for a very good reason. It has been found that they are diametrically opposed to any molecules which combine soap and water. Their bodies have the ability to repel all cleansing agents and aids, with the obvious exception of the dog's tongue.

Boys can get dirty washing the dishes. The fact that there is enough bacteria under their nails to start a small but virulent plague, does not concern them in the least. We know perfectly well why our son aspires to be a gladiator when he grows up. He suspects that they never take off their armor, and therefore never have to take a bath.

Is it in the best interest of this hungry child with matted hair and yellow teeth to appear at school three hours late every day? Is society prepared to handle the weight of the plague that will surely ensue as an entire elementary school full of this type of specimen arrive daily?
Sincerely,
A Concerned Parent

I've swallowed a lot of garbage from child psychologists, but this I'm tempted to make them eat.
My question is this. If someone really has a sure fire strategy for successful child development, why don't they just share this sage advice with the kids? Why entrust mothers with yet another lofty concept of parenting, which is clearly over our heads? As for me, I've decided to place this imaginative little tale down on the

children's bookshelf, next to Winnie The Pooh. As children's stor-
ies go, this one is a classic.

CHAPTER 19

MOTHER'S DAY: THE FINAL FETE

Mothers are truly an endangered species. They just haven't gotten around to listing us yet. One of the practices that threatens to wipe us out completely is the celebration of Mother's Day. It all started years ago when some greedy greeting card manufacturers, candy manufacturers, clothing manufacturers, florists and restaurant owners who had it in for their moms, got the idea that it might be fun to coerce people to express their appreciation for EVERYTHING that their mothers have ever done or given to them in one day. This is a monumental task to expect of one day, not to mention one mother.

Never-the-less, you would have to be some sort of sloth, not to want to participate in what has become one of our most cherished rituals. Schools send home lovingly prepared indigestible "Cookbooks" and hand made bric-a-brac to add to your already overstocked shelves. This includes the ever popular plaster of Paris handprint of your child. The original version, done in dirt and magic marker of course is still hanging on your walls.

To honor her, the Queen For A Day will be served breakfast in bed. This meal is ritualistically carried up on a bed tray, and proudly presented to Her Majesty who by this time is cowering under her bed trying desperately not to notice all the crashing, screams and threats emanating from her kitchen. The chefs line up at mom's bedside for approval. And as hungry little eyes devour her every facial expression, she musters up the courage to take the first bite. That's all she'll ever get. After all, what real mom could eat a whole meal in front of her starving little children? While everyone else is busy finishing off the masterpiece, mother slinks into the kitchen to survey the disaster which she inherited along with the throne.

If you ask me, someone is going to have to do something about this day. Mothers spend hours and fortunes driving their offspring around town helping them to select the perfect presents to surprise them with. We landscape ourselves with floral dresses, flowered hats and flower corsages until we look like front lawns. We develop varicose veins waiting for hours on lines at overcrowded restaurants that run out of what we want to eat before we even get there.

The alternative to this, would be for mom to whip up an absolutely gourmet meal for her adoring ones. A meal mind you, which will take about six hours to shop for, cook, serve, and clean up after. Heaven forbid that you just send out for pizza!

I ask you. In which fetid swamp do they spawn the type of invertebrate who would add to a mother's already exhausting schedule, by insisting upon her running herself ragged glorifying herself? All we really want on this day is what we already have; those who conferred upon us the title of "Mother". What we really need however, is some extra time to accomplish the chores associated with that title.

Let some greeting card Grinch come up with that sort of a gift, and I guarantee that person would make a fortune.

CHAPTER 20

HOW I FAILED SUPERMARKET 101

I remember the exact day that I went shopping and came home with three bars of deodorant soap, a decorating magazine, and a potted plant. I went in with a list long enough to justify taking out another mortgage on the house. These were the only three items however, which I felt confident would not destroy our planet, or cause my family to expire before my coupons did.

The supermarket became my library. I spent more time reading labels than I spent reading all the newspapers and magazines that we subscribe to. In order to understand what you were investing in, it would have helped to hold a PhD in nutrition with a minor in molecular chemistry. Between calories, sugar, fat, carbohydrates, sodium, and potassium content, not to mention food additives, allergens, hormones and insecticides, I didn't have to watch my cholesterol. I could have to worried myself into a stroke. And what is so bad about preservatives? At my age I could use a preservative.

Remember how Mrs. Cleaver (yes, The Beaver's mom) set salutatory standards of motherhood with her baked goodies? My son who has acquired standards more rigid than the FDA, the

USDA and the American Cancer and Heart Associations would no sooner consider eating the inside of a Twinkie than taking a bath. I clearly remember Ozzy and Harriet serving grilled hot dogs and potato salad without worrying that their blood pressure would shoot higher than their ratings. Today, only a Wicked Queen would hand Snow White an apple that was not organically grown.

Americans applauded while pure cardiac arrest, dripping with tradition, flowed from Aunt Bea's kitchen. Before the "energy crunch" became a nutrition bar, my mom confidently served her family TV dinners. Today, my kids would add up the calories in that meal, factor it, divide that figure by the nutritional content, multiply by the additives and preservatives, and reduce that figure to the nearest significant digit. They would then begin to consider the chemicals used to manufacture the packaging materials. By then they would have lost their appetites.

Before PCB's, detergent had a good name, and the worst that you could get from smoking was a spanking. As children, we were on first name basis with our bologna. Aerosol hairspray reigned supreme over beehive hairdos, and the "greenhouse effect" had the decency to remain under glass panels in the yard. Drinking water came out of the sink faucet, and flour did not seem less wholesome just because it was bleached. Salt made food taste good, and no one cared if it iodized or not. Natural fibers referred to our clothing, and nitrates and triglycerides were used in explosives. And isn't coconut oil used in tanning solutions?

Suddenly a shout rang out from aisle three.
"I've found it", a female voice rang out. "It contains no salt, sugar, fats or preservatives! and it's 100% fiber!"
"What is it?" I demanded as I steered my shopping cart around a quick u-turn and charged towards her aisle.
"Athletic socks!" she answered triumphantly.

As I stumbled to the check-out counter mumbling to myself, trying to decide whether I wanted to die of caffeine poisoning or of the chemicals used to remove it, I came upon a poor broken pathetic figure of a young mother slumped over her shopping cart. Waving her shopping list like a white flag of surrender, she confessed to everyone within earshot that she could not remember if soy was good or bad. And while I couldn't help her either, I helped myself to a fashion magazine from the rack. At least it wouldn't poison anybody.

CHAPTER 21

IT'S NOT FAIR!

O ur elementary schools view the annual Science Fair as an opportunity for mothers to help pique their youngster's intellectual curiosity; our own having been sedated during the past eleven months of lolling about watching soap operas and eating chocolates. This is supposed to be our chance to broaden our education instead of our hips, while facilitating our child's moment of scientific achievement. I have done my own impartial survey and have determined that parents as a whole look forward to this event, the way they look forward to a case of chicken pox.

My statistics show that one out of every three moms suffers severe loss of self-esteem and self-confidence over this exercise. It has been known to reduce otherwise confident women to tears, and has sent some of the more timid of us back to our analysist's couch. The fact is, that it doesn't matter how much money you earn, how many miles a day you jog, or how many hours per week you put into community service. This event is THE EQUALIZER. Pass, and you will be rewarded with the sweet fulfillment of remaining a player in your child's education. Fail, and you will be filled with guilt that you passed up an education in nuclear physics just to get married and give this child life.

I personally keep a stock of lab supplies in our garage that would make the FBI suspicious, and the US Dept. of Agriculture positively green with envy. Madame Curie discovered radiation under more primitive conditions than my kids have in our home laboratory. Among the beakers, graduated cylinders and Bunsen burners lies my pride. Not to mention the remnants of previous experiments:

- 3 one-gallon jugs of liquid plant fertilizers (we only needed a tablespoon of each for the entire experiment).

- A canister containing 12 packages of flower and vegetable seeds - now mixed, unfortunately.

- 12 corroded pennies. One might have been a nickel at one time.

- Several petri dishes containing something that will either cure cancer, or wipe out the entire world (in which case we no longer have to worry about the former).

- An empty ant farm. All the ants managed to successfully find their way into the house

- A homemade rat maze, which the rats figured out before I did.

Prior to my introduction to the school Science Fair, I could list my scientific experiences on the back of a piece of litmus paper. To date however, I have nearly roasted to death trying to determine how hot it can get inside a commercial clothes dryer. I once gained ten pounds trying to identify different flavors of cool-aid while blindfolded. I have wiped out half of my collection of baby teeth trying to ascertain the effects of various drink sweeteners on them. I have hosted every creature imaginable in my home, and have spent months trying to persuade some of them to leave. One year I helped dye 300 dog biscuits various colors in an attempt to discover which dogs prefer. Apparently dogs are color-blind, and our son prefers brown.

While I realize that there are proteins out there that are far more complex than I am, I could just imagine the new list of suggested projects for next year's fair:

- Visit a live volcano and measure the amount of lava flow from one single eruption. Remember, metric measurements get the judge's attention!

- Engineer a simple microorganism which could have a major impact on a global scale. Remember, microorganisms are not permitted in school. You will have to bring a photograph of your microorganism

- Determine what the geology of the world will be by the year 5,000 AD, using the Continental Shift theory. A full size replica would add extra points to your score.

- Build a new software program for the next generation of computers. Note: the judges frown upon common forms of computer language and no swear words will be tolerated.

- Determine mathematically if it is possible that we have overlooked a heavenly body. You may confine your search to our solar system. Extra points will be awarded if it can support intelligent life.

- Develop a new automobile fuel and build a simple model prototype for your demonstration. Please do not use any flammable materials as they are against the school's safety code.

- Using state-of-the art techniques in genetic engineering,

build a small animal or plant, which in your opinion could become a valuable member of the earth's food chain. You must be ready to defend your opinion. Note: You may order ready-made genes, as you are being judged solely on the sequencing of the genes and upon the value of the organism that you produce.

It's not as though I scorn scientific inquiry. It's just that I can't seem to get excited over projects that hold such little relevance for me. The things that I really want to know are never addressed. Things such as:

• How much longer can a fifteen year old washing machine last?

• How much dirt is actually good for a child to consume over one lifetime, and is it ok for the child to consume it all in one day?

• Why is it that a one-pound box of candy can put seven pounds of weight on a woman?

I realize that I can't be trusted with the formula for ice, but any member of the family of green leafy vegetables could recognize the significance of the following projects on the world:

• I would like someone to devise a toothpaste that not only prevents cavities, but actually reverses those in progress and works whether or not the child actually uses it.

• I would like a mirror that shrinks my facial pores and wrinkles instead of magnifying them. Extra credit if the reverse side could reverse gray hairs.

• How about a lipstick that won't melt in the dryer? A gum?

·   How about an all-in-one product that permanently re-
moves zits, bad breath, and magic marker?

Let's face it. The entire concept of a Science Fair could justify
itself if only one entry was a formula, not a prototype mind you,
but just a formula for world peace. One that could end disease,
poverty, world pollution, illiteracy, prejudice and apathy, and actually helped restore the ozone layer. Of course, it would have to
be simple enough for a child to understand, so that even our pol-
iticians could endorse it.

After considerable analysis, research, and observation, I have
come to the following conclusion. This year we are simply going
to count the number of seeds in a seedless watermelon or two. It
won't win and go on to the big District Competition, but at least
it's one we could all swallow.

CHAPTER 22

THE HAND THAT ROCKED THE BOAT

The Equal Rights Movement has been blamed for having accomplished little but perpetrating egotistical women, demasculated men, undisciplined children and awful music. In Cropduster, Ohio, where it is still fashionable for a woman to drive a tractor, wives were unaware of the advances that a then small, obscure group of women fought for on their behalf. They were too busy patching the roof, slopping the pigs, rearing their children, balancing the checkbook, and even going out to sell semi truck parts to provide extra money for their families, to notice that they were excluded from masculine occupations.

As the feminist movement gained public awareness and some validity, the activists could be heard singing their oppressed little hearts out all across the land. In Cropduster, mothers were too busy fighting scourges in nature to mull over how liberated they wished that they could be. They were too busy rebuilding their tornado-demolished houses to follow the political triumphs that a group of dedicated zealots were accomplishing on their behalf. As the woman's movement spread and gained full recognition in Washington DC, the excitement escaped the women of Cropduster. They were too busy nursing their babies to question why it was that they were chosen to procreate instead of men. They were too preoccupied helping their husbands with the planting and the harvesting to mull over the inequality of their existence.

The pendulum began to swing as the Equal Rights Amendment was introduced. Liberated mothers began leaving their children with caretakers and came out of their closets in double-breasted jackets and fedoras. They won scholarships and furthered their educations. The school system responded to the political climate. There was an emphasis on instructing young girls in science and math. Banks responded. Women were given loans to open businesses and became entrepreneurs. They rose to high corporate positions, and began to insist on entry into social organizations formally reserved only for men. Women made the transition from kitchen cabinets to government posts.

In Cropduster, mothers continued to serve on PTA committees and church boards. They continued to be the primary educators of their children and their husbands' main support system. They organized lifesaving blood drives, fundraisers to feed the starving, and shelters for the homeless. They studied political issues, voted in elections, and guided their local leaders from behind political platforms. They took their families to church and prayed for the world as well. They were blissfully unaware that their contributions to society were unimportant, their positions menial.

And although the ERA failed to pass into law, all around the country women began to stand on equal footing with men. They became as poorly paid and as overly taxed as the men. They developed signs of stress and chemical dependencies formally more associated with their male counterparts. They started to suspect that they were carrying two full time careers when they returned home from their jobs to find their tidy households in shambles. They sent their children to analysts to try to figure out why they felt so neglected, their need to be heard reflected in their blaring angry music.

The mothers of Cropduster read about their newly gained status with some degree of trepidation. They began to raise some very poignant questions. "Now that we are liberated", they wondered, "what is meant by the expression, "women and other minorities"? Have they taken a census? Does equality mean that we will ALWAYS be right, even when history, logic and even calculators contradict us? And when we do change our minds, will we astound ourselves with our own flexibility instead of just admitting that we'd been wrong? Does it mean that we should now go completely berserk when another driver gets in our way? Will we stop using road maps and instead wander aimlessly lost about strange towns for hours, even days, too pigheaded to ask for directions? Does equality mean that we will be expected to bond with our children and each other by making rude sounds with our armpits and leaving behind us sickening gaseous odors when we leave a room? Will we no longer require two deodorants in order to stay "daisy fresh" all day long? Will we now be looked upon as muscular instead of plump? And will we finally become distinguished as we age instead of matronly?

In Cropduster, Ohio, where women continue to have the babies, run their households, help run their farms, supplement their husband's incomes, still find time for political and spiritual issues, and devoting themselves and their talents to their communities, things have not changed one bit since the Equal Rights Movement. Maybe they should have paid more attention right from the beginning. Obviously the essence of it completely eluded them. Because in Cropduster, Ohio, a mother's place is still where it always was. Simply, in charge.

CHAPTER 23

MY SECRET IDENTITY

Sixteen years ago I lost something rather valuable to me: my identity. I know that I placed it down right next to our first child's birth certificate. I hadn't even missed it until the other day. Then it hit me that I could spend an entire day identifying myself as someone's mother, someone's wife, someone's friend, someone's daughter or even, someone's owner, without ever using my own name.

My husband calls me "honey", the kid's call me "mom". At the check-out in the supermarket I'm known as "ma'am". Letters addressed to me read "Mrs". What people call me behind my back I'd rather not even know. Sometimes I think it was a waste of energy for my parents even to have named me. After all, I can be identified by my social security number. I also have a number on my driver's license, an address, a number on my library card, and I get a new one every time I visit a fast food restaurant. The telephone company can identify me by my phone number, and I can also be accessed by the digits on my credit cards. The other day, the butcher calld me "number four". I'd have preferred to have been called a "ten".

Our oldest daughter who seems to have acquired a degree in

psychology somewhere along the line had a theory.
"Mom, you are suffering from an identity crisis." she said confidently.
"Well", I countered," I wear more labels than a garment on the clearance rack, why shouldn't I get a little confused?"

"No need to spaz mom." She enunciated this sentence slowly enough so that an English language learner could get it.
"By your age you'd think that you'd get used to it".
Witch.

"Look", I countered, speaking to the chair. She had already flown off on her broomstick. When you were little I was Santa Claus, the Tooth Fairy, the Easter bunny, and a Leprechaun on St. Patrick's Day. When your sister was born who do you think played the Stork?" I yelled back, at no one.
"You're too tall to be a Leprechaun", she chided out of one side of her mouth as she popped a zit in the bathroom mirror.
"Yea, well it just so happens that with all these identities I could be in danger of developing a split personality", I whined. "I wouldn't even know how to feed a crowd like me."
"Try a buffet", came the overly compassionate answer. Now WHO did this child sound like anyway?

"Do you realize that I could single-handedly overload an elevator, or put a swimming pool at maximum capacity"? No answer. She'd locked herself inside her hovel and was probably brewing up a potion.

Still, I mused to myself, I do cringe when asked to identify myself. Maybe I could get a job again, like I had before the children? At least that would give me a little independence. But then, I'd be someone's secretary, boss, nurse, teacher. OMG! THIS COULD GO ON! And it would only add to my confusion, I thought miserably.

If only I could jog my memory a bit, I'm sure that I could find me somewhere inside this labyrinth of labels. Let's see. My Ego, which had suffered a lump in it's existential throat after twenty three years of marriage and four children is right here, next to my Conscience. My Ego looks a little smaller than I had remembered it. My Conscience, on the other hand, got quite a bit larger. Probably well fed by my newly acquired Spiritualism. Well, would you look at this!? Here's my Identity after all! I hadn't even recognized it, it has grown so much! It seems that all of my traits have coalesced and formed a compilation, which is now who I truly am! I hadn't lost my identity at all, I had broadened it over the years of emotional growth and maturation. It sure was a relief to find myself again.

"Are you ok mom?", as she emerged from her sanctuary and asked in a gentle, caring tone.
"Of course I am dear", I had to smile at the sweetness of her compassion.
"Oh, good!" she said with a relieved little laugh. "Sometimes I swear that you're losing your mind!"

CHAPTER 24

A CROWN CONTENDER

My mother put Mr. Clean to shame. I had my doubts about a man who shaved his head and hung out behind a toilet bowl. Mom took water stains on her furniture personally. I completely washed out when it came to house cleaning. I considered dusting to be a rearrangement of dust particles. Visitors to my parents house stuck to the plastic covers on her couches. Mine stuck to the gum and candy on my chairs. Mom buried her head in the laundry basket and viewed collar rings a reflection of failure. I sent shirts to the cleaners, and gave myself a "A" if I remembered to pick them up. While mom won bed making contests with her housekeeper, I had to search for my bed which was usually buried underneath the wash. On Thursdays mom ironed everything, down to our underwear. It was rumored that I could scream loud enough to straighten the seams in a pair of pants and once used her ironing board as a sled.

A totally organized woman, mom arrived everywhere on time, and planned her own headaches. I was fashionably late for everything and caused everyone else plenty occasion for headaches. Mom had lists for everything. She would list what she needed to buy at the stores, what she was going to prepare for meals, whom she owed letters to, and what she wanted to mention to me the next time I called from college. I jotted things down on the back of birthday cards and mailed them. I took notes in class on my sleeves, and lost test answers in the laundry.

In labor, mom had general anesthesia and swore she would never have another baby. I had natural childbirth and swore at everyone. Mother read cookbooks from cover to cover, digested the contents, made notes in the margins, and extolled the virtues of vinaigrette. In her
refrigerator there was never a green that wasn't fresh enough to replant. I am a "born again" cook. My ministry is to leftovers. I give homage to ham, genuflect in the presence of limp vegetables, and have a pious devotion to left-over anything hat can be made into my famous "garbage soup".

Mother rose to Vice President of the Ladies Club of our local VFW. I distinguished myself by helping my husband sew banners for children's soccer and soft ball teams. After 3 children mom hired a housekeeper so she could share her talents with her community. After four children I hired a nanny and did the same. I never learned how to pin a cloth diaper. Mom forgot how to.

In the Maternal Derby I had always considered myself a contender for the crown. But the crown was not what I had expected. It contained thorns. Along with the joys of marriage and the hopes and triumphs of motherhood, came the tears the fears and the pain. I had to have my own children to understand my mother's compassionate love for hers. I had to see her with my children to realize how selflessly she loved me. In the times of agonizing indecision and in those that require maddening patience, I turned to the woman who, in her wisdom, wouldn't tell me that childbirth would hurt. Nor that it would be just the training ground for the main event; bringing those children up. The crown that mothers pass on to their children is the courage, strength and love that they teach us by example, and the ability to laugh a bit at ourselves and at life. Our very survival depends on it.

ABOUT THE AUTHOR

Susan Chiofalo

Susan wrote a column called
"Tell Me About It" for a local
newspaper "The Valley Star" in
Canyon Lake, California, in
1990. The publisher told Susan,
he would copyright the column
back to her, because he thought
she was talented, and that she
might want to write a book
someday. She started writing
the book "MOTHERS, AN EN-
DANGERED SPECIES" in 1992, 35
years after marrying her sweetheart Vincent, in 1968. 28 years
after writing the book, it was

published by VAC PUBLISHING. Susan and Vincent currently re-
side in Baja California, Mexico.

Made in the USA
Las Vegas, NV
27 May 2022

49430344R00059